"Although Vernon Robbins is one of the most erudite New Testament scholars today, he writes here from his heart in language that anyone can understand. He traces the central Christian theme of love through the New Testament, showing how different writers developed the concept with their distinctive emphases. Together these emphases contribute to a fuller picture of how the New Testament invites us to love others."

—CRAIG KEENER
F. M. and Ada Thompson Professor of Biblical Studies, Asbury Theological Seminary

"This wonderful, encouraging book draws readers into the flow of the wisdom of love in the New Testament. Robbins shows in striking and beautiful ways the development from the wisdom of ancient Israelite and Jewish texts to the deep love for one another that never ends, that binds things together in the turbulence of human existence. The wisdom and power of love flow from this book into readers' minds, hearts, and souls."

—ROY R. JEAL
Professor Emeritus, Booth University College

"Pack your bags for a textual journey! An expert explorer of ancient texts, Vernon K. Robbins offers readers an accessible and highly personal journey through early Christian texts looking for love. Along the way he encourages us to 'nurture love wherever we can.' This is scholarship in the service of our shared humanity—scholarship that provides resources for living in flourishing human communities."

—ROBERT H. VON THADEN JR.
Professor of Religious Studies, Mercyhurst University

"With a personal perspective and a conversational tone, Robbins guides the reader on an exploration of love across the New Testament. The journey is filled with historical, literary, and rhetorical insights on how love functions in various books of the Christian canon. The reader comes away with a sense of both the distinctive role of love in various books and the profound ways that particular configurations of love are creatively related to one another."

—BART B. BRUEHLER
Director of Biblical Studies, Uniting College for Leadership & Theology, South Africa

"If you want to think about love in the New Testament profoundly and from new perspectives, Vernon Robbins here gives you a golden opportunity. Presented as a journey of discovery, he engages his readers at every destination with a unique blend of scholarly observation and personal reflection. Anybody can take the journey and not be lost, and scholars will be surprised that the journey takes so many surprising twists and turns. This expedition traverses the New Testament revealing how early Christians understood their newfound love in Jesus Christ."

—DUANE F. WATSON
Professor Emeritus of New Testament Studies, Malone University

"Vernon Robbins's *Finding Love* is a wonderful exploration of this most fundamentally important theme in the New Testament—interspersed with his intriguing reflections on his own life story and the contemporary situation. The book will be useful for many readers including adult education classes, college classes, and certainly for New Testament scholars."

—JOHN GRANGER COOK
Professor of Religion, LaGrange College

Finding Love

Finding Love

A Journey Through the New Testament

VERNON K. ROBBINS

CASCADE *Books* • Eugene, Oregon

FINDING LOVE
A Journey Through the New Testament

Copyright © 2025 Vernon K. Robbins. All rights reserved. Except for brief quotations in critical publications or reviews, no part of this book may be reproduced in any manner without prior written permission from the publisher. Write: Permissions, Wipf and Stock Publishers, 199 W. 8th Ave., Suite 3, Eugene, OR 97401.

Cascade Books
An Imprint of Wipf and Stock Publishers
199 W. 8th Ave., Suite 3
Eugene, OR 97401

www.wipfandstock.com

PAPERBACK ISBN: 979-8-3852-6051-5
HARDCOVER ISBN: 979-8-3852-6052-2
EBOOK ISBN: 979-8-3852-6053-9

Cataloging-in-Publication data:

Names: Robbins, Vernon K. (Vernon Kay), 1939–, author.
Title: Finding love : a journey through the New Testament / Vernon K. Robbins.
Description: Eugene, OR: Cascade Books, 2025. | Includes bibliographical references.
Identifiers: ISBN: 979-8-3852-6051-5 (paperback). | ISBN: 979-8-3852-6052-2 (hardcover). | ISBN: 979-8-3852-6053-9 (ebook).
Subjects: LCSH: Agape. | Love—Biblical teaching. | Love—Religious aspects—Christianity.
Classification: BV4639 R62 2025 (print). | BV4639 (epub).

Unless indicated otherwise, the quotations of the Bible are from the *NRSVue Holy Bible, New Revised Standard Version, Updated Edition.* National Council of the Churches of Christ in the United States of America, 2021. All italics in biblical texts have been added by the author.

VERSION NUMBER 103125

Contents

Abbreviations | VII
Preface | IX

Introduction | 1

1 Glimpses of Divine Love in Mark | 8
2 Loving One's Enemies as Reshaped Torah in Matthew | 25
3 Loving One's Enemies as Prophetic Wisdom in Luke | 41
4 *Christ* Jesus as God's Love in Letters of Paul | 59
5 Love, Life, and Friendship in the Gospel of John | 78
6 Cosmic Peace, Church, and Love in Colossians | 96
7 Cosmic Church, Love, and Mystery in Ephesians | 107
8 God is Love in 1 John | 116

Conclusion | 129

Books for Further Reading | 137

Abbreviations

auth. var.	author's modification of the NRSVue (unless another version indicated)
auth. trans.	author's translation
LXX	Septuagint (Greek) version
trans.	Translation by

Preface

THERE ARE SO MANY people for whom I am thankful as I type a few last words before submitting this manuscript. Thanks to my faithful Zoom audience while COVID-19 was doing its evil work from March through November in 2020. I will always be grateful to you for those Tuesdays and Fridays we spent together. Your encouragement and love have made this whole project possible.

Special thanks to Cynthia Thompson, who asked me during Fall 2022 to teach the chapter on the Ten Commandments in a book on Moses for The Forum class at Shallowford Presbyterian Church. I was unsure I had recovered enough from a period of post-retirement depression in 2022 to start teaching again, but this was the beginning of a new community of love for me. Along with the amazing leadership of Rev. Anna George Traynham and her remarkable colleagues at Shallowford, I am once again leading a happy and active life. When Cynthia and her co-leader Brad Bryant became aware I was writing a book on Love in the New Testament, they asked if I would teach my chapters after Easter in 2023. The excitement and encouragement of the wonderful people in this class helped me complete a draft of the manuscript by the end of June. I am ever so grateful.

A hearty thanks to members of the Faith Seeking Understanding class, which meets next door to the Forum class. When Robert Dean and Catherine Taylor discovered I was teaching about Love in the New Testament, they asked if I would teach them during the Fall. When I accepted, many deeply probing questions and comments brought refinement and depth to the thoughts-in-progress in my revisions at the time. Thank you.

Extraordinary thanks to Roy R. Jeal for his exquisite editorial suggestions in each chapter. Any existing errors are likely to be in text I added later and he has not seen. Also I am deeply grateful to Wayne Coppins for

Preface

sending me a copy of his beautiful translation of Oda Wischmeyer's *Love as Agape* when he knew I was studying love in the New Testament.

Transitions are always challenging. Going through them with my loving wife Deanna has made it all possible. How could I be so fortunate!

July 2025
Vernon K Robbins

Introduction

A JOURNEY WITH LOVE

THIS IS A BOOK about love that is a road trip through the New Testament. You are invited to take this journey with me. Why take such a journey? The concept of love did not suddenly spring up fully formed in early Christianity. Rather, it emerged slowly here and there, and gradually it took center stage in certain sections of the New Testament. As a result, there are large portions of the New Testament where the concept of love does not occur. We will see how love first lingers in the background, then has its special moments, and finally becomes a fully formed concept.

Recently I have read *Breakfast with Buddha, Lunch with Buddha,* and *Dinner with Buddha,* and also I have reread *Zen and the Art of Motorcycle Maintenance.* Each of these books takes the reader on a road trip. In the midst of my reading I also reread *God: A Biography,* which is a journey through the Jewish Hebrew Bible (Tanakh) in dialogue with the arrangement of the books in the Christian Old Testament. The Christian Old Testament ends with prophetic books so the Christian story of Jesus flows naturally out of prophecy. In contrast, the Tanakh places the Prophets immediately after the Torah (Genesis through Deuteronomy) so they call God's people to obedience to the 613 commandments (*mitzvoth*) in the Torah.

So how will our journey proceed? I must tell you at the beginning I intermingle some of my own journey while writing this book with the journey we will take together through the New Testament. At the end of summer in 2019 I retired from Emory University, after fifty years of teaching biblical studies. When the COVID-19 pandemic hit, the groups I was leading could no longer meet in-person. To accommodate a member of my writing group who had moved to Virginia, I had learned how to use Zoom during spring 2020. When COVID hit, a friend at Emory who had become highly proficient with Zoom was happy to answer my questions as I began to expand my use of it. On March 24, 2020, I started a Tuesday–Friday Zoom class on "Human and Divine Love in the New Testament." After the last session on Tuesday, November 17, 2020, I decided to reshape the study guides for those sessions into reader-friendly chapters for adults who may simply be interested in the subject, or who may be deeply invested in the subject as part of their religious life.

FROM COVID-19 TO THE PRESENT

When we started the Zoom journey on March 24, 2020, COVID-19 was just gathering steam to do its frightful work. We started with the Synoptic Gospels—Mark, Matthew, and Luke—and I discovered that this is a good way to start. When our journey ended with 2 Peter on November 17, 2020, we were still in COVID isolation.

During 2021 my life was dominated by caregiving responsibilities for a blind ninety-six-year-old woman whom we had gotten into assisted care in April 2020. When she passed away in June 2021, I became executor of her will in addition to attempting to arrange for her funeral and life celebration during COVID, which we finally managed in November. This created many situations where I saw *agapē* love in action. By the end of December I was completely burned out and collapsed into significant depression. I began to long for new days of happiness. Little by little, with the help of loved ones and others, days of happiness began to emerge.

There was a wonderful dinner celebration on the fourth of July in 2022 with two couples along with their children who are very dear to us, some of whom brought girlfriends into our family gatherings, and now two of them are married couples. Then there was the amazing evening when the Atlanta Master Chorale presented "The Ways of Stars." Happiness flowed through my body during the performance. I longed for the happiness never to stop. Then there was the evening of the oral performance of the first half of T. S. Eliot's *Four Quartets* interwoven with two Beethoven Concerti performed by the Emory Vega String Quartet. By September 11, 2022, I began writing, and the words began flowing freely from my fingertips. God is good and happiness is present once again in my life. But now Vladimir Putin in Russia is waging a horrible war against Ukraine, Israel is now devastating Gaza

Introduction

and parts of Lebanon and Syria, and China is more and more a concern both economically and militarily. Is there any way that studying love in the Bible can confront and treat emerging feelings of despair about these things?

HOME IS WHERE LOVE STARTS

In preparation for writing this book, I went to Pitts Theology Library at Emory University to find recent books on love. I found some and have listed them in the *Books for Further Reading* at the end of this volume. One of the books is John C. Peckham's *The Concept of Divine Love in the Context of the God-World Relationship*. Peckham says that "those who respond positively to God's love will in fact enjoy an everlasting reciprocal love with God." This sentence jumped off the page for me.

My parents taught me as a child that all of life and every blessing comes from God. For some reason I never realized this meant they had started me on a journey of "an everlasting reciprocal love *with* God." Despite their flaws, and there were many, and despite my flaws, and there are many, they launched me on a journey of everlasting reciprocal love, and I am so grateful for this. This journey is a thread that runs from my earliest boyhood days to my present days. I can see now that this thread holds my difficult days together with my happy days.

God continually gives me life and healing, and I have no choice but to thank God for it. In addition, I experience ongoing, everlasting love from my wife Deanna. I am truly fortunate, right? My wife is a major gift of God's reciprocal love to me. I am only sorry not all marriages can be as filled with love as full, inspiring, and enriching as ours has been and still is. I know there are many other happy marriages, and I am thrilled about this. So I am not supposing ours is the only marriage blessed by wonderful love. I simply am grateful that this is part of God's reciprocal love with me.

Why am I interested in all the nuances of meaning of love? Is it because as I grow older I see love as a tender touch, a sweetly-spoken word, or a shimmering inner experience of intimacy and gratitude. As a way to begin, let us think a bit about three basic kinds of love: *eros*, which is sexual; *philia*, which is friendship; and *agapē*, which is selfless. In the midst of this, there is much talk about *agapē* love as somehow central to Christianity. What about *philia* and *eros*? Do some Christians think there is a problem with sexual love, even though they participate happily and gratefully in it?

And what about friendship? Does friendship have any special meaning in Christianity, or is friendship simply a secular relation between people? And what about *agapē*? Is *agapē* simply selfless? Can only God give selfless love? There are many questions here, and we will try to explore them in a manner that invites dialogue among people who enjoy a lively discussion while learning new concepts of love in the Bible.

LOVE AS CONCEPT AND TRADITION

Love is a well-known concept within Greek mythology and philosophy, and it is a well-known concept in the Bible of Israel. When the New Testament emerged during the first century CE it gave love a noticeable Christian configuration. The recent comprehensive book by Oda Wischmeyer, *Love as Agape: The Early Christian Concept and Modern Discourse*, published in German in 2015 and in English in 2021, supports a renewal of discussion and debate among New Testament scholars about the emergence of *agapē* love as a Christian concept and tradition.

The approach in this book you are reading enacts Oda Wischmeyer's interpretive strategy of "from tradition to innovation" in a manner designed for a broad audience of explorers. This means that each book in the New Testament receives meanings of love from Israelite, Jewish, biblical, and philosophical practices, debates, and writings and builds on these meanings in new ways. This is an exciting way to enter the history of Judaism and Christianity that moves century by century to our own context for thinking about love in our present world. So just as I and others moved through our journey of studying love in the New Testament during 2020 while vaccines were being discovered and administered to fight COVID-19, the people of Israel and then the earliest Christians lived through challenging, and even devastating, times as they were discovering and putting into action their concept of love.

It is often asserted that *agapē* love is central to Christianity, but how much evidence is there that love is central to Christianity? You may be interested to know that *agapē* love occurs in some form three hundred twenty times in the New Testament. I say *in some form*, because the Greek stem *agap-* can occur as a noun, verb, adjective, or participle. If you look closely at these words in the letters of Paul, you see there are more occurrences of the noun *love* (*agapē*) than some form of the verb *to love* (*agapān*). Does this mean the *concept* of love is more important than *acts* of love in Paul?

Introduction

If you look at words for love in the Gospel of John, you will see that some form of the verb *to love* (*agapān*) occurs more frequently than the noun *love* (*agapē*). So are *acts* of love more important than the *concept* of love in the gospel of John? We will address these issues in due course. For now, let us broaden our thoughts about love to help us understand our journey a little better.

The goal of the present book is to enable an audience of explorers who may or may not know extensive things about the Bible to experience the way major writings in the New Testament make love into a "Christian" concept and tradition. You may know about *agapē* love especially from hearing 1 Corinthians 13 read at weddings. But you may find it interesting to explore the concept of love in a non-specialist way throughout other portions of the New Testament.

So, what did I learn about love in the New Testament during those eight months of Zoom sessions? My biggest surprise was that no noun or verbal form of *agapē* love occurs in the book of Acts, which is the second longest book in the New Testament after the gospel of Luke.[1] After we complete our journey through the occurrences of *agapē* love in the New Testament, I will reflect a bit on the absence of *agapē* love in the twenty-eight chapters of the book of Acts. But for now let us keep our eyes on where *agapē* does occur in the Bible.

We will begin in the first chapter with the gospel of Mark, where love hides in the mystery and confusion of the coming of the kingdom of God but is nevertheless present. The second chapter focuses on Matthew, where love comes into the world on the wings of the Torah and the Prophets. The third chapter focuses on Luke, where Jesus' prophetic blessing of the poor and marginalized and announcement of the burden of wealth introduces a pathway through loving one's enemies and praying for those who persecute you. The fourth chapter focuses on Paul, where wisdom, a hidden mystery decreed before the ages, is revealed through love in the crucifixion and resurrection of Christ and is personified through people who build up believing communities. The fifth chapter focuses on the gospel of John, where God's love flows into the work in the cosmic energy of life in God's Logos Son. The sixth chapter focuses on the Pauline letter of Colossians, which envisions cosmic peace and love in the church. The seventh chapter

---

1. Acts contains 18,451 Greek words, Luke 19,482, https://catholic-resources.org/Bible/NT-Statistics-Greek.htm. The adjective beloved (*agapētos*) occurs once in plural form when Acts 15:25 refers to "beloved Barnabas and Paul," and this is the only occurrence of an *agap-* stem word in this very long and important book.

focuses on Ephesians, where God's love creates a new humanity in Christ's church, and where people are made alive with Christ and raised together with Christ. The eighth and final chapter is on the first letter of John, where God's love becomes a central, fully formed concept. Then a concluding chapter will summarize our journey together through the New Testament and add some final reflections.

CONCLUSION

In this introduction we have packed our bags in preparation for a journey through the New Testament looking for love. We are ready to take the first steps in our journey. You have learned some important things about me and my goals as I am writing this book. You have also learned that the opening phase of our journey will take us on a search for love in the mystery and confusion of the coming of the kingdom of God. As we journey we will remember that a major goal of our activity is to claim love in our own lives. As we explore together, we will nurture love wherever we can. Exploring love in the New Testament has already helped me renew and celebrate love. My hope is that renewal and transformation will grow and expand your life as we travel together on this journey.

QUESTIONS FOR DISCUSSION

1. In your view, what does *agapē* love mean? Do you think *agapē* love is love between two or more people? Do you think *agapē* love only occurs between humans and God?

2. Do you think *agapē* love is human love or divine love? If it is human love, can God have *agapē* love? If it is divine love, can humans have *agapē* love?

3. Do you think there is a direct connection between *agapē* love and happiness? If so, how are they connected? If they are not connected, explain why they are not?

4. Do you think *agapē* love is a duty? Or is *agapē* love something a person *chooses* to do or not to do?

5. Do you think *agapē* love is a gift? If so, who is the giver of the gift of love and who receives the gift of love?

Introduction

6. What are your thoughts about the absence of *agapē* love from the book of Acts in the New Testament, which is the primary source for information about the earliest years of Christianity?

1

Glimpses of Divine Love in Mark

> And he said to them, "To you has been given the secret of the kingdom of God, but for those outside, everything comes in parables."[1]

IT IS SURPRISING HOW hard it is to find love in the gospel of Mark. Love hides in the hustle and bustle of Jesus' proclamation of the coming of the Kingdom of God. It is difficult even to find clarity about the Kingdom of God in Mark. Jesus announces at the beginning of his ministry that the kingdom is at hand and all should repent and believe in the good news.[2] But what is the relation of this to the love of God? I will argue in this chapter that love is "hiding in the wings" in Mark. Indeed, I will argue that this is the nature of the "secrecy" that follows Jesus from early in the gospel to the very end of it.

Love is so tangled up in Mark that what may look like love actually is not love and what does not look like love actually is love. Undoubtedly the greatest example of something that looks like love but is not love is kissing. There is one moment when someone kisses another person. You probably have already guessed what it is: Judas kissing Jesus to betray him to the chief priests, scribes, and elders.[3] There is no other instance of kissing. I will discuss what does not look like love but actually is love as we proceed.

1. Mark 4:11.
2. Mark 1:14–15.
3. Mark 14:44.

Alongside the entanglement of love in confusing thoughts and actions, there is no mention of friendship throughout Mark. Jesus commands people to follow him, and this is how he gathers twelve disciples. At times Jesus takes three or four of his disciples with him.[4] Large crowds gather at certain points in the story. These people are regularly amazed at what happens. But there is no indication that any of them becomes Jesus' friend.

One of the noticeable things about the gospel of Mark is secrecy. On some occasions, Jesus does not permit the demons to speak, because, our narrator tells us, they know who he is.[5] Twice it says demons know Jesus is the Son of God.[6] Jesus tells a healed leper not to say anything to anyone, but the healed man goes out and openly proclaims anyway.[7] Jesus tells his disciples they have been given the secret (mystery) of the kingdom of God while all other people receive things only in parables (riddles).[8] He also tells them nothing is secret except to come to light.[9] After Jesus raises a twelve-year old girl from death to life, he strictly orders his disciples and the parents of the girl that no one should know this.[10] Jesus tells a healed blind man to go directly to his home rather than through the village so no one will see him.[11] When Jesus asks the disciples who they think he is and Peter answers he is the Messiah, Jesus orders them not to tell anyone about him.[12] After Peter, James, and John see Jesus transfigured on the mountain, Jesus orders them to tell no one what they have seen.[13]

In the context of this secrecy Jesus' disciples progressively find it more difficult to understand Jesus. They do not understand what was happening in the feeding of the five and four thousand.[14] When Jesus tries on three different occasions to explain to his disciples that he must go to Jerusalem and be killed there, they not only do not understand what he is saying but they

---

4. Mark 5:37; 9:2; 13:3; 14:33.
5. Mark 1:34.
6. Mark 3:12; 5:7.
7. Mark 1:44–45; cf. 5:18–20.
8. Mark 4:11.
9. Mark 4:22.
10. Mark 5:43.
11. Mark 8:26.
12. Mark 8:30.
13. Mark 9:9.
14. Mark 6:52; 8:17–21.

FINDING LOVE

resist it and become angry about it.[15] After the Passover meal with Jesus in Jerusalem and their time with Jesus when he prays in Gethsemane, when Judas betrays Jesus to the chief priest, scribes, and elders with a kiss, all the disciples desert Jesus and flee.[16] Peter follows along to the courtyard of the high priest, but then he denies he has any relationship to Jesus by telling a servant-girl he does not "know or understand" anything she is talking about.[17] After Jesus is crucified and buried, when women come to Jesus' tomb, find it empty, and are told that Jesus has risen and is not there, "they said nothing to anyone, for they were afraid."[18]

This dimension of secrecy in Mark is regularly called "the messianic secret," and there have been many scholarly discussions and arguments about it since I started serious study of Mark during the 1960s. During the evening of November 20, 2022, while I was walking almost three miles to get much needed exercise, I was thinking about this chapter on Mark. Suddenly it occurred to me that what is called "the messianic secret" in the gospel of Mark is really a different secret than the history of scholarship has been able to perceive. The gospel of Mark tells us more about Jesus than I was able to see until this moment in my walk. What is it that is *really* hidden in the gospel of Mark? I invite you to walk along with me on the journey that has brought me to a different conclusion than the traditional one that usually is given.

As I have already mentioned above, there is no discussion of friendship in Mark, and there is no embracing or kissing, except Judas's kiss of betrayal. In addition, there is no occurrence of the noun *agapē* in the earliest gospel in the New Testament. In the sixteen chapters of Mark there are five occurrences of a verbal form of *to love* (*agapān*) and three occurrences of the adjective *beloved* or *much loved* (*agapētos*). Overall, this is not many assertions of love. But when love words do occur in Mark, they are strategic and have strong influence on Matthew and Luke who used Mark as a source when they wrote their gospels.

There is no occurrence of the verb to *love* until we get to the middle of the gospel of Mark. In chapter ten a man runs up to Jesus, kneels before him, calls him "Good teacher," and asks him what he must do to inherit

---

15. Mark 8:32; 9:32; 10:41.
16. Mark 14:50.
17. Mark 14:68.
18. Mark 16:8.

eternal life.[19] Jesus says to him, "Why do you call me good? No one is good but God alone. You know the commandments: 'You shall not murder; You shall not commit adultery; You shall not steal; You shall not bear false witness; You shall not defraud; Honor your father and mother.'"[20]

When the rich man calls Jesus "Teacher" and tells him he has kept all these commandments from his youth, our narrator tells us Jesus looked at him, *loved* (*ēgapēsen*) him, and said, "You lack one thing; go, sell what you own, and give the money to the poor, and you will have treasure in heaven; then come, follow me."[21] How can it be that suddenly Jesus is moved by *love* to call this rich man to follow him, but the rich man is so attached to his wealth that he cannot sell it and follow Jesus? Why has the narrator suddenly described Jesus in this way, when there has been no mention of *love* in all the preceding stories where Jesus has been with his disciples and when Jesus has healed people? This is what I mean by "*love* hiding in the wings" in Mark. It never appears for nine chapters, but suddenly the narrator describes Jesus as *loving* a rich man who will not make the necessary sacrifice of his wealth to follow him as a disciple.

If we go back two chapters in Mark to Jesus' first prediction of his death and resurrection, Jesus expands on the meaning of death and resurrection in terms of "following," which is regularly called discipleship. In order to become a disciple, Jesus says, people must "deny themselves," take up their cross, and follow him.[22] As Jesus expands on this he reasons, "For what will it profit them to gain the whole world and forfeit their life?"[23] The man in chapter 10 came to Jesus asking him what he must do "to inherit eternal life." When Jesus responds to him, he is rewording his earlier assertion about "denying oneself" in relation to the man's exceptional wealth. Mark has Jesus speak out of *love* to the rich man that he must go, sell what he owns, give the money to the poor, and he will have treasure in heaven, and he adds, "then come, follow me."[24] It appears that Mark is giving the reader a small glimpse of *love* in Jesus that is difficult even for us to see. It doesn't immediately look like *love* when Jesus tells the rich man that he must go, sell what he owns, and give the money to the poor. But we must

19. Mark 10:17.
20. Mark 10:18–19.
21. Mark 10:20–21.
22. Mark 8:34.
23. Mark 8:36.
24. Mark 10:21.

notice that he adds "and you will have treasure in heaven." The man came to Jesus asking about eternal life, and Jesus has responded to him out of *love*. If we ask, "but what then will the man do, because he has no way to support himself," the answer is that he should come and follow Jesus.

So in Mark, because Jesus *loves* the rich man who comes to him asking what he must do to inherit eternal life, Jesus tells him *the gospel* as it is presented in the gospel of Mark. This *gospel* is not a story filled primarily with joy and happiness. Rather, it is a story of Jesus' death and resurrection that is so challenging that the disciples are unable to understand it while they are with him on earth. It is only after his death and resurrection, while they themselves are preaching the gospel to all nations and being handed over to councils, beaten in synagogues, and standing before governors and kings[25] that they will come to understand how this gospel speaks of receiving eternal life.

If we think Jesus' call to the rich man to follow him is not a satisfactory answer, we need only read further in Mark. We know that after Jesus tells the rich man what he must do to receive eternal life, the man is shocked and goes away grieving, for he has many possessions.[26] Wouldn't it have been wonderful if this man had followed Jesus and replaced Judas who betrayed him! But this is not how the story goes. Instead, the rich man goes away and Jesus explains to his disciples how hard it is for those who have wealth to enter the kingdom of God.[27] When the disciples are perplexed, Jesus expands his explanation by explaining that people cannot save themselves, but what is impossible for mortals is possible for God.[28]

At this point Peter speaks up, as he often does in Mark, saying, "Look, we have left everything and followed you." And Jesus responds, "Truly I tell you, there is no one who has left house or brothers or sisters or mother or father or children or fields for my sake and for the sake of the good news, who will not receive a hundredfold now in this age—houses, brothers and sisters, mothers and children, and fields, with persecutions—and in the age to come eternal life. But many who are first will be last, and the last will be first."[29] This would seem to be a statement by Jesus in Mark about how God's *love* functions deeply hidden in the gospel of denial of one's life. Jesus,

25. Mark 13:9–10.
26. Mark 10:22.
27. Mark 10:23.
28. Mark 10:27.
29. Mark 10:29–31.

however, does not talk about it as *love*, and *love* may not readily come to mind as Jesus talks about eternal life in this way. But isn't it appropriate to say that *love* is hiding in the wings here? Or would it be more proper to say it is hiding in the dark, namely the darkness of denial of home and brothers and sisters and mother and father and children and fields. If this is a gospel of *love*, it is a kind of *love* very difficult to understand. Can we blame the disciples if they have considerable confusion about it?

Two chapters later in Mark the reader finally comes upon a significant discussion of *love*. Indeed, four occurrences of verbal forms of *love* (*agapān*) suddenly appear in one place. When a Jewish scribe comes to Jesus asking him which commandment is first of all, Jesus responds by saying the first commandment is "Hear, O Israel: the Lord our God, the Lord is one; *you shall love* (singular: *agapēseis*) the Lord your God with all your heart and with all your soul and with all your mind and with all your strength."[30] Finally, *love* appears when Jesus is teaching someone! Or is he teaching? In truth, Jesus isn't telling the scribe anything he doesn't already know. Jesus may be emphasizing something in a way the scribe has not exactly thought about before. But Jesus is simply reciting the Shema, which every Jew learns as a child and is told to repeat every day. In Hebrew, *shema* means *hear*. What Jesus recites to the scribe is called the Shema because it begins with "Hear (*shema*), O Israel." Some Jews recite the Shema in the morning, at noon, and in the evening, or perhaps even five times each day.

The Shema is in the sixth chapter of the last book of the Torah, Deuteronomy, where Moses is presenting the final commandments, statutes, and ordinances to the people of Israel before he dies and they gradually enter the land of Canaan (modern-day Israel). None of this is new to the scribe or to Jesus. Jesus is simply showing what he learned about *love* growing up as a Jewish boy. Immediately after reciting the Shema in Deuteronomy Moses says, "Keep these words that I am commanding you today in your heart. Recite them to your children and talk about them when you are at home and when you are away, when you lie down and when you rise."[31] In other words, Moses has said, "Learn these words by heart and do them." Then Moses tells them to recite them regularly to their children so they also learn them by heart. In addition, he says to put these words on their doorposts, which Jews put as a *mezuzah* at the front door of their house. Perhaps most important for us is the insight that Jesus not only learned

30. Mark 12:29–30.
31. Deut 6:6–7.

these words *by heart,* but he *put love* for God in his heart and *kept love* for God in his heart.

Then Jesus said, "The second is this, 'You (sg.) shall *love* your neighbor as yourself.' There is no other commandment greater than these." After Jesus says this the scribe says, "You are right, Teacher; you have truly said that 'he is one, and besides him there is no other'; and 'to *love* him with all the heart and with all the understanding and with all the strength' and 'to *love* one's neighbor as oneself'—this is much more important than all whole burnt offerings and sacrifices."[32]

It is not surprising that the scribe would say Jesus is right that to *love* God is the first commandment. But it is surprising the scribe would include in this commandment *loving* one's neighbor as oneself. The scribe could have called Jesus' attention to the appearance of *loving* one's neighbor in another book of the Torah (Leviticus) instead of its being included in the Shema. But by the time of Jesus many Jews did join them together. Even more surprising is the scribe's assertion from the Prophets that *loving* God and one's neighbor are *more important* than burnt offerings and sacrifices.[33] This scribe is thoroughly on board with Jesus' emphasis both on *love* of God and *love* of neighbor so that he presents thoughts out of the Prophets as well as the Torah.

Here, then, *love* explicitly surfaces in Jesus' teaching, but it appears in discussion with a Jewish scribe rather than one or more of the disciples. When Jesus responds to the scribe by telling him he is "not far from the kingdom of God,"[34] Jesus is embedding *love* of God and *love* of neighbor deeply in the coming of the kingdom of God. But exactly how does this *love* function in the coming of God's kingdom? The answer does not easily appear in the gospel of Mark, and the disciples are so confused and disturbed by what is happening that they do not get near to it. Is God's *love* in the coming of the kingdom working in such a way that it is driving Jesus toward death in Jerusalem? This certainly does not look like any traditional understanding of *love,* or does it?

---

32. Mark 12:31–33.
33. Cf. Isa 1:11–17; Mic 6:6–8.
34. Mark 12:34.

JESUS, GOD'S BELOVED ONE: LOVE AS A DIVINE PASSIVE ADJECTIVE

In order to understand the meaning of *divine love* in Mark we must go a step further, namely to the adjective *beloved* (*agapētos*). There are only three occurrences of the adjective *beloved* in Mark, but they are strategic occurrences, namely they show a particular strategy of the writer of Mark. The adjective *beloved* occurs: (1) at the baptism of Jesus; (2) at the transfiguration of Jesus; and (3) in a parable about a vineyard in which the vineyard owner sends his "beloved son" to collect the share of the owner's produce. The secret that Jesus is beloved is first told to Jesus alone,[35] secondly to four of Jesus' select disciples,[36] and thirdly it is embedded in a parable.[37] The reader sees all three of these occasions, but in each instance the words about Jesus *being loved* do not bring God's *love* for Jesus *clearly out into the open*. A major reason is that God's *love* is hidden in the divine passive adjective *agapētos*. But this calls for further explanation.

Before going to the baptism, the transfiguration, and the parable we must understand something about the adjective *agapētos*, which is regularly translated *beloved* or *much loved*. In this adjective, God's love is hidden in what can be called a divine passive expression. Many will know that Jews regularly do not speak the name of God, which is present in the four letters YHWH. These letters must not be spoken aloud as a special word. So, many Jews *circumlocute* (talk around) the name of God by referring to God as Ha Shem (the Name), or the Most High, or the Blessed One. But also they may use a *divine passive* to refer to God. Perhaps the prime example of a divine passive in the New Testament is the creedal reference to "he *was raised* on the third day in accordance with the scriptures."[38] Everyone knows this means that God raised Jesus on the third day. Indeed, it means that YHWH raised Jesus on the third day. But the creed avoids saying the name of God by using the *passive* verb "was raised [by God]." In other words, it is easy for us to forget that the earliest people we call Christians were Jews who believed that Jesus was the Messiah. These believing Jews continued to follow many speech patterns to which they were accustomed. In Mark, the adjective *beloved* functions as a divine passive adjective describing Jesus

---

35. Mark 1:11.
36. Mark 9:7.
37. Mark 12:6.
38. 1 Cor 15:4.

as the Son *whom God loves*. So let us recap where we are in our journey through Mark.

What seems clear is that Mark highlights interaction between human and divine *love* through Jesus who proclaims the kingdom of God and then submits to God's will. A key result is a difficult journey for Jesus's disciples. God's *love* for Jesus is very important in Mark, but this *love* is embedded in a web of mystery, secrecy, confrontation, confusion, frustration, and lack of understanding by the disciples. This web of mystery is the kingdom of God. We will not solve the mystery of the kingdom of God in Mark. But our journey can show us the story framework that Mark established for his gospel and that Matthew and Luke took into their gospels. This framework can help us as we encounter surprising new dimensions of *love* in the other gospels and writings in the New Testament.

THE BAPTISM AND TRANSFIGURATION OF JESUS

So now let us continue. The gospel of Mark has no occurrence of a passive form of the verb *to love* (*agapān*), which could have been a way for the author to write. But it has three occurrences of the passive adjective *agapētos* meaning *beloved [by God]* or *much loved [by God]*. Let us go back to the beginning of the story in the gospel of Mark. Immediately after the opening verses, John the Baptizer appears,[39] and people come from the entire Judean countryside and from Jerusalem for forgiveness of sins through repentance and baptism in water. Then Jesus comes from Nazareth of Galilee to be baptized by John. As Jesus is coming out of the river Jordan, he sees the heavens split apart, and the spirit descends like a dove on him. Then a voice comes from heaven declaring divine *love* upon Jesus as a son in whom God is well-pleased.[40] Here God's statement to Jesus sounds like YHWH's voice in Psalm 2:7 to one being enthroned as king of Israel "I will tell of the decree of YHWH: He said to me, "You are my son; today I have begotten you." But it also sounds like God's statement to Abraham, "Take your son, the *beloved* one (*ton agapēton*) Isaac, whom you *love* (*ēgapēsas*), and go into the land of Moriah and offer him there as a burnt offering on one of the mountains that I shall show you."[41] In addition, it sounds like the words of YHWH later in the Abraham story, "By myself I have sworn, says YHWH, because

---

39. Mark 1:4.
40. Mark 1:11.
41. Gen 22:2 auth. var.

Glimpses of Divine Love in Mark

you have done this, and on my account have not spared your *beloved* son (*ton huiou sou to agapētou*), surely blessing I will bless you, and multiplying I will multiply your seed as the stars of heaven, and as the sand which is by the shore of the sea, and your seed shall inherit the cities of your enemies."[42] A journey through the gospel of Mark suggests that all of these aspects of YHWH's voice have implications for the story of Jesus as told in this gospel. Our interest at the moment is the particular assertion by God's voice that Jesus is *loved* by God as a special son.

It is not common to think of the gospel of Mark as a gospel of *love*. There is good reason for this. As we have seen, words for divine *love* are not very frequent in its sixteen chapters. But when the adjective *much loved* or *beloved* (*agapētos*) comes directly out of heaven to Jesus in the eleventh verse of the gospel, we understand that this is a strategic statement about God's *love* for Jesus. This adjective occurs sixty-one times in the New Testament, but most of the time it refers to people we might consider to be *ordinary* humans. In the eleventh verse of the gospel of Mark this adjective is used by the voice of God speaking directly to Jesus Messiah calling him God's *beloved* son.

To see the importance of this declaration by God's voice at the beginning of the story, let us travel to the middle of Mark's story[43] where Jesus takes three of his disciples—Peter, James, and John—up on a high mountain apart from all other people. Suddenly Jesus is transformed before the disciples and his clothes become dazzling white, beyond any whiteness any kind of bleach could produce on earth. In other words, Jesus' form changes into a "heavenly" form. Regularly this is referred to as the *transfiguration* of Jesus. When Jesus is in this heavenly form, Elijah appears with Moses, and they talk with Jesus. Peter also speaks to Jesus, suggesting that three booths be built—one for Jesus, Moses, and Elijah—but the narrator says Peter didn't know what else to say, because all of them were terrified.

Elijah and Moses died many years before the time of Jesus, of course. But the Old Testament tells how Elijah ascended into heaven in a whirlwind.[44] And sometime during the emergence of Christianity, perhaps as early as the first century CE, a Jewish writing known as *The Testament of Moses* recounted the ascension of Moses into heaven. This writing probably did not exist at the time of the writing of Mark around 70 CE, but Mark

---

42. Gen 22:16 LXX auth. trans.
43. Mark 9:2–8.
44. 2 Kgs 2:11.

presupposes a view that Moses also at some point was taken into heaven and dwells there along with Elijah, Enoch, and others who were taken into heaven at the time of their deaths. The mountain to which Jesus took the three disciples obviously reached to the opening of heaven. This made it possible for Elijah and Moses to meet and talk with Jesus at the opening of heaven on the top of the mountain to which Jesus had gone with three of his disciples.

After Peter's suggestion that three booths should be built,[45] a cloud overshadows Jesus and the disciples, and a voice says, "This is my Son, the *Beloved*, listen to him!" A major difference between this event and the baptism is that by the middle of the story Jesus has disciples. When Jesus takes this inner circle of disciples with him up on a high mountain, they themselves hear the divine voice of God tell them that God *loves* Jesus and they must listen to him!

Why the cloud? In Exodus when Moses and the Israelites first entered the wilderness of Sinai, Yahweh told Moses, "I am going to come to you in a dense cloud, in order that the people may hear when I speak with you and so trust you ever after."[46] Then at a later time Yahweh descended in the cloud and stood with Moses on the top of Mount Sinai.[47] As God stood with Moses, God made a covenant with Moses and all the Israelites[48] that contained the ten commandments and special ordinances for living within the covenant.

When God comes in a cloud that overshadows Jesus and the three disciples the story of God's presence is continuing from the time of Moses and Elijah to the story of Jesus. During this event, Peter, James, and John hear God refer to Jesus with an *agapē-* adjective that refers to God's *love* of Jesus as his special son. In addition, God's voice tells them to *listen to him*. But do the disciples hear the voice as a statement of God's *love*? Or for that matter, do even we hear it as a statement of God's *love*? We notice that God calls Jesus "the Son of God," but do we hear the part that says God *loves* this son? If we do not hear it, one of the reasons is that God's *love* is hiding in the divine passive adjective *agapētos*.

---

45. Mark 9:5.
46. Exod 19:9.
47. Exod 34:5.
48. Exod 34:10.

GLIMPSES OF DIVINE LOVE IN MARK

THE PARABLE OF THE WICKED TENANTS

As we journey forward three chapters beyond the transfiguration of Jesus we see the third and final occurrence of the adjective *beloved* in Mark. And here it occurs in a parable! Jesus spoke to his disciples about parables back in chapter 4, and we overhear the discussion. There he tells the disciples that they have been given the *secret* or *mystery* of the kingdom of God, but "for those outside" *everything comes in parables*. We hear Jesus tell this to his disciples, but are we ourselves ready to hear how the mystery of the kingdom of God is *hidden* in *parables*?

At the beginning of the twelfth chapter of Mark, Jesus began to speak "in parables" to people listening to him in Jerusalem. Jerusalem, of course, is where Jesus will soon be crucified by Roman soldiers. Jesus does not speak openly to the people in Jerusalem about his death and resurrection, as he does to his disciples in 8:31; 9:31; and 10:32–34. Rather he tells them about his death *in a parable*.[49] The parable is about a vineyard owner who leased his vineyard to tenants and went away to another country. At first the owner sent slaves to collect from the tenants his share of produce from the vineyard, and the tenants seized them, beat them, and sent them away empty-handed, and they even killed some of them.[50] Finally the owner sent his *beloved* (*agapētos*) son to the vineyard, feeling certain the tenants would respect him. Instead, the tenants seized him, killed him, and threw his body out of the vineyard.[51]

After telling the parable, Jesus asked the crowd, "What then will the owner of the vineyard do?" Then Jesus answers his own question: "He will come and destroy the tenants and give the vineyard to others," and he recites to the audience the scripture, "The stone that the builders rejected has become the cornerstone; this was the Lord's doing, and it is amazing in our eyes,"[52] which are the words of Ps 118:22–23. It seems clear that this parable rehearses the history of God's people in terms of a *beloved* son who "has come" and whom the tenants will kill (namely, Jesus). But do we readily see that here Jesus is predicting his death in Jerusalem *in a parable* to the people who will soon see him killed?

---

49. Mark 12:1–12.
50. Mark 12:2–5.
51. Mark 12:8.
52. Mark 12:10–11.

Once we have learned about *agapētos* as a divine passive adjective, we can hear the divine voice at the baptism and transfiguration of Jesus saying that God *loves* Jesus. But here God's love for his son is hiding so deeply *in a parable* that even we might miss it. When we hear Jesus quote from Psalm 118 that "The stone that the builders rejected has become the cornerstone?" and "this was the Lord's doing, and it is amazing in our eyes,"[53] it may become clear to us that Jesus is *the beloved son* in the parable. Still there is a lot here that even we cannot be absolutely clear about, right? If this is God's *love*, it still is a huge challenge for anyone to understand it fully and clearly.

CONCLUSION

In this phase of our journey together we have learned that for the most part in the gospel of Mark *love* hides in the secrecy and mystery of the coming of the kingdom of God. *Love* comes explicitly into view when a scribe asks Jesus what commandment is first of all and Jesus answers by reciting the well-known Jewish Shema about *loving* God and then adds a second commandment about *loving* one's neighbor. The surprising thing is that the scribe praises Jesus for his correct answer and then adds "this is much more important than all whole burnt offerings and sacrifices."[54]

The result of the dialogue between Jesus and the scribe is two occurrences of the verb *agapān* with reference to human *love* for God and two more occurrences referring to human *love* for their neighbor. But then we must recall one more thing. When Jesus praises the scribe for answering wisely he says, "You are not far from the kingdom of God."[55] As we have journeyed together about this, I have mused that here Jesus seems to be directly linking the coming of the kingdom of God with the actions of *loving* God and neighbor. In other words, when a person *loves* the Lord God of Israel with all their heart, soul, mind, and strength, and *loves* their neighbor as themselves, they are near to the kingdom of God just as the kingdom of God is near to them. We have observed that, for the most part, the double-focused *love* by humans within the coming of the kingdom of God is hidden in Mark. Indeed, it is a mystery that may intentionally be a "secret" that will only in due time come fully into view, because "there is

---

53. Mark 12:10–11.
54. Mark 12:33.
55. Mark 12:34.

nothing hidden, except to be disclosed; nor is anything secret, except to come to light."[56]

At this point, it may be appropriate for us to notice something Jesus does *not* say. In Mark, Jesus never says that God *loves* those who love him, nor does Jesus ever say that God *loves* the world. We have noticed, however, that God's *love* is hiding in the wings of the coming of the kingdom of God. As the fulfillment of time approaches in the imminent coming of the kingdom,[57] God speaks directly to Jesus saying, "You are my Son, the *Beloved*; with you I am well pleased."[58] Here, as we noticed earlier, God is using his "hidden presence" in the passive adjective *beloved* to say, in essence, "You are my Son, I *love* you and I am well-pleased with you." Since this happens in the first chapter in Mark, Jesus knows from the beginning of the story that God *loves* him, but no one has heard this except Jesus and us, the readers!

When we get halfway through the story, Jesus takes his innermost circle of Peter, James, and John, up on a mountain, where they see Jesus transfigured, are overshadowed by a cloud, and hear God's voice saying, "This is my Son, the *Beloved*; listen to him!"[59] Again God's *love* is "hidden." It is hidden in the passive adjective *beloved* and in a cloud! But, nevertheless, *secretly* Peter, James, and John have been told that God *loves* Jesus and they must listen to him. But can they truly *hear* it? By this time in the story they are baffled by virtually everything Jesus himself has done and what has happened around him. In addition, Jesus "ordered them to tell no one about what they had seen, until after the Son of Man had risen from the dead."[60] This immediately diverts their attention from the divine voice about God's *love* for Jesus to what "this rising from the dead could mean."[61] So, in no way are the disciples going to come readily to the realization that God *loves* Jesus and will somehow take care of him. And if they had recognized that the language of *beloved* was present in the story of the near sacrifice of Isaac, what would they have thought? That God would at the last minute not let Jesus die? The disciples are confused, and it is not entirely their fault.

56. Mark 4:22.
57. Mark 1:15.
58. Mark 1:11.
59. Mark 9:7.
60. Mark 9:9.
61. Mark 9:10.

Finding Love

Very puzzling things are happening around Jesus, and Jesus is doing very unexpected things.

Since we as readers know how the story ends, we may think the disciples also should have known the end of the story. But the purpose of Mark's story is to take us on a journey through the incredible confusion that surrounded Jesus' life and death in a context where Jesus said the kingdom of God was near at hand. And does the kingdom of God clearly come at the end of the story? Well, perhaps we want to say it clearly has come in the message of the young man in the tomb that Jesus "has been raised" and that the disciples and Peter will "see him" in Galilee "just as he told" them.[62] But is this *clear evidence* that the kingdom of God *has come*? Does it not still remain *significantly unclear* how the kingdom of God may have come in all of this and exactly what this might mean about God's *love*? Isn't God's *love* still significantly hidden in all of this?

Despite all this confusion in Mark, can we appropriately say we think we can see God's *love* hidden in the warp and woof of this gospel? Perhaps we are pushing the boundaries very hard to say this. But we do have two more pieces of evidence. The first is that Jesus *loved* the rich man who came to him asking what he must do to inherit eternal life.[63] So, in the midst of Jesus' activities, God's gift of *love* to Jesus enabled Jesus to *love* this rich man who came to him. But this feels unsatisfactory, doesn't it, when Jesus' *love* for the man does not empower him to transfer his *love* from his possessions to following Jesus.[64]

But there is a second piece of evidence about God's *love* in a parable. Just where we should expect to find it in Mark, right? Jesus tells a parable in Jerusalem about tenants of a vineyard who seize, kill, and throw out of the vineyard the *beloved* son of the owner of the vineyard.[65] And the people "realized that he had told this parable against them."[66] As skillful readers we can see a *hidden reference* to Jesus, whom God *loves*, right? Still, though, God's *love* remains very hidden even here, doesn't it?

Doesn't it seem accurate to say that our journey through Mark has shown that God's *love* is hovering here and there in the story, but still it is quite hidden? We said at the beginning of this chapter, "It is surprising

---

62. Mark 16:6–7.
63. Mark 10:21.
64. Mark 10:22.
65. Mark 12:8.
66. Mark 12:12.

how hard it is to find *love* in the gospel of Mark." We have found some *love* there, and now it is important to say how significant this *love* is. In Mark we hear two prime commandments that we must *love* the Lord our God and we must *love* our neighbor as ourselves. But also we have seen how God speaks his *love* for Jesus, albeit in a passive adjective that hides God as the subject. So Mark is not only about Jesus as Messiah son of God,[67] but Jesus as *Beloved* son of God who, like his Father, does it all for love, in the context of *agapē* and *agapētos*. Jesus himself is following the first commandment and the second. In this framework we see that God's *love* is present with Jesus throughout all that he does and all that happens to him. Because of the presence of God's *love* for Jesus, Jesus can focus on his activity of healing, teaching, calling, and then on suffering and dying. These are Jesus' tasks, and he fulfills them within a framework of God's *love* for him as part of the coming of the kingdom of God.

As we move forward on our journey it will be instructive to see how Matthew and Luke expand Mark's sixteen-chapter story of Jesus into twenty-eight chapters (Matthew) and twenty-four chapters (Luke). Part of this expansion includes elaborating the topic of *agapē* love. I invite you to follow on the journey to the other synoptic gospels, both which used the gospel of Mark as a written source as they expanded the story of Jesus.

QUESTIONS FOR DISCUSSION

1. We know Jesus grew up as a Jewish boy. What happened in his boyhood that enabled him to state the first part of his answer to the scribe so quickly in Mark 12:29–30? If you have difficulty answering this, see what it says in Deut 6:4–7.

2. Compare Mark 12:29–30 with Deut 6:4–7 and explain a major aspect of Jewish belief and practice that contributed to Jesus becoming a *loving* person by the time he was an adult.

3. On the basis of Mark 9:7, where God speaks from the cloud saying to three of Jesus' disciples, "This is my son, the *beloved*, listen to him!," do you think Jesus' disciples should have known God's special *love* for Jesus during their time with him? If you think they should have known, explain how they could have known. If not, why not?

---

67. Mark 1:1.

4. When you hear the story Jesus told about tenants of a vineyard who killed the *beloved* son of the owner when he was sent to collect the owners share of produce from the vineyard, do you naturally think about God's love for Jesus? If so, why? If not, why not?

5. Do you think the writer of Mark had a special goal in emphasizing mystery, secrecy, and hiddenness on the one hand and misunderstanding and confusion on the other hand as he presented the story of Jesus? If so, explain.

6. Do you think the gospel of Mark is an example of a passive form of writing that expresses the life of its author in an indirect way? In other words, do you think the author of Mark himself may have had some of the confusion and uncertainty that the disciples and even the women at the tomb exhibit in Mark? If so, explain.

7. Do you think it is better for the gospel of God's *love* to emphasize mystery and hiddenness, or is it better for the gospel of God's *love* to be as open and explicit as it is possible to make it? Explain the pros and cons of a *mystery and hiddenness* approach.

2

Loving One's Enemies as Reshaped Torah in Matthew

Jesus said, "But I say to you: Love your enemies and pray for those who persecute you."[1]

IN THE PREVIOUS CHAPTER we found God's love hiding in the mystery and confusion of the coming of the kingdom of God in Mark. This love remains significantly hidden in Jesus' activity of calling disciples, healing people, suffering, dying, and rising. We concluded that we found God's love for Jesus especially at the baptism, where Jesus hears the voice of God, and the transfiguration, where three of Jesus' disciples hear the voice of God.

When we come to Matthew in this chapter, we see God's love coming into the world on the wings of the Torah and the Prophets. In Matthew, Jesus teaches like the Pharisees teach, updating and reshaping the Torah and the Prophets on the basis of new challenges God's people face. A special aspect of Jesus' teaching is about God's love. Jesus' teaching about love reaches a highpoint in the Sermon on the Mount, where it reshapes some of the ten commandments and reaches its highest requirement in *loving* one's enemies. A major question in Matthew is who Jesus considers to be the major *enemies* his followers must love. As we ask this question we will also ask ourselves who our enemies are whom we must love. We get some clues

---

1. Matt 5:44.

in Matthew about the enemies Jesus' followers must love, but who are the enemies Jesus calls us to love? Will reshaping the Torah and the Prophets in the Old Testament help us to see how we are to love our enemies? We will ask these questions both of the gospel of Matthew and of ourselves as we journey through Matthew's way of presenting Jesus' teaching about love.

FULFILLMENT OF THE LAW (TORAH) AND THE PROPHETS

The first thing we need to remind ourselves about the gospel of Matthew to understand how loving our enemies comes into Jesus' teaching on the wings of the Torah and the Prophets is to remember how Matthew often says about an event that "this took place to fulfill what had been spoken through the Prophets," followed by the recitation of one or more verses of scripture in the Old Testament. This happens five times in the opening chapters of Matthew as it tells about Mary bearing a son to fulfill the promise, "the virgin shall become pregnant and give birth to a son,"[2] the Messiah will be born in Bethlehem to fulfill, "you Bethlehem . . . from you shall come a ruler who is to shepherd my people Israel,"[3] Jesus' parents flee to Egypt to fulfill, "Out of Egypt I have called my son,"[4] Herod decrees that all children two years old or under will be killed to fulfill, "A voice was heard in Ramah, wailing and loud lamentation,"[5] and Jesus' parents make their home in Nazareth when they return from Egypt to fulfill, "He will be called a Nazarene."[6]

MATTHEW'S REWRITING OF MARK'S GOSPEL

Matthew used the gospel of Mark as a source and reproduced the two Markan instances of the adjective *agapētos* meaning *beloved* in the baptism and transfiguration of Jesus. At the baptism in Matthew, God does not speak only to Jesus, as he does in Mark, but speaking in third person he identifies Jesus aloud by saying, "This is my Son, the *Beloved*, with whom

---

2. Matt 1:22–23.
3. Matt 2:5–6.
4. Matt 2:13–15.
5. Matt 2:16–18.
6. Matt 2:23.

I am well pleased."⁷ Since John the Baptist is standing nearby, it appears that he would have overheard the divine voice announce that Jesus is his Son whom he *loves*. At the transfiguration in Matthew, the divine voice in the cloud announces the same thing to Peter, James, and John, but adds "listen to him" as it also does in Mark.⁸ In Matthew the cloud is described as *bright* or *shining*, which may reflect knowledge of a passage in the Greek Old Testament like Exod 16:10, which says that the *glory* (*doxa*) of YHWH appeared in the cloud when Aaron spoke to the congregation of Israelites. In the transfiguration, when the disciples hear the voice, they fall to the ground and are overcome by fear. But Jesus comes to them, touches them, and tells them, "Get up and do not be afraid."⁹ In Matthew, then, Jesus' healing touch shows the compassion he has for the three disciples who are with him. Matthew builds into his story, therefore, God's *love* for Jesus in the passive adjective *agapētos* at Jesus' baptism and transfiguration, and Jesus shows compassion for his disciples when they are afraid. And how does this compassion come to expression in Matthew?

In addition to Matthew's retelling of Mark's stories of the baptism and transfiguration, Matthew also tells, with slight modifications, the Markan story of the man who asks Jesus about the most important commandments. In Matthew the man is a lawyer rather than a scribe as he is in Mark, and he questions Jesus in front of Pharisees and Sadducees *to test him*. Instead of asking Jesus which is the *first* commandment, the lawyer asks Jesus which is the *greatest*. Jesus responds without including the Shema introduction "Hear, O Israel: the Lord our God, the Lord is one" as in Mark 12:29. This leaves simply a commandment which says, "You shall *love* the Lord your God with all your heart and with all your soul and with all your mind," to which Jesus adds, "This is the greatest and first commandment." Then he continues as in Mark with, "And a second is like it, 'You shall *love* your neighbor as yourself.'" But then in Matthew Jesus adds, "On these two commandments hang all the Law and the Prophets."¹⁰ Here we see the special emphasis on the law (Torah) and the Prophets in Matthew.

---

7. Matt 3:17.
8. Mark 9:7//Matt 17:5. Mark 9:7, however, omits "in whom I am well pleased."
9. Matt 17:6–7.
10. Matt 22:37–40.

RESHAPING THE TORAH AND THE PROPHETS IN MATTHEW

The fulfillment of statements in the Prophets in the earliest stories and in multiple places throughout Matthew establishes the environment for Jesus' teaching about love through the Torah in the Sermon on the Mount, which is a three-chapter speech Jesus presents to the large crowd that gathers at the beginning of his preaching, performance of healings, and calling of disciples.[11] This sermon features mountain imagery like in Exodus[12] and is a reshaping of Moses' teaching on Mount Sinai in Exodus 20 and 34. After Jesus opens his sermon with a series of beatitudes,[13] he reconfigures six commandments in the Torah with a pattern of, "You have heard that it was said . . ., But I say to you. . ." (see the table below).

Jesus starts with, "Do not think that I have come to abolish the Law (Torah) or the Prophets; I have come not to abolish but to fulfill."[14] Then he begins to update and reshape commandments in the Torah by saying:

> You have heard that it was said to those of ancient times, "You shall not murder"; and "whoever murders shall be liable to judgment." But I say to you that if you are angry with a brother or sister, you will be liable to judgment; and if you insult a brother or sister, you will be liable to the council, and if you say, "You fool," you will be liable to the hell of fire.[15]

---

11. Matt 4:12–25.
12. Matt 5:1; 8:1.
13. Matt 5:3–12.
14. Matt 5:17.
15. Matt 5:22.

Loving One's Enemies as Reshaped Torah in Matthew

> ### Reshaping of Torah in Matthew's Sermon on the Mount
>
> **Do not think that I have come to abolish the Law or the Prophets; I have come not to abolish but to fulfil . . . For I tell you, unless your righteousness exceeds that of the scribes and Pharisees, you will never enter the kingdom of heaven.**
>
> You have heard that it was said to those of ancient times, *"You shall not murder"*; and *"whoever murders shall be liable to judgment."*
>
> **But I say to you** that if you are angry with a brother or sister, you will be liable to judgment, and if you insult a brother or sister, you will be liable to the council, and if you say, "You fool," you will be liable to the hell of fire. So when you are offering your gift at the altar, if you remember that your brother or sister has something against you, leave your gift there before the altar and go; first be reconciled to your brother or sister, and then come and offer your gift. Come to terms quickly with your accuser while you are on the way to court with him, or your accuser may hand you over to the judge and the judge to the guard, and you will be thrown into prison. Truly I tell you, you will never get out until you have paid the last penny.
>
> You have heard that it was said, *"You shall not commit adultery."*
>
> **But I say to you** that everyone who looks at a woman with lust has already committed adultery with her in his heart. If your right eye causes you to sin, tear it out and throw it away; it is better for you to lose one of your members than for your whole body to be thrown into hell. And if your right hand causes you to sin, cut it off and throw it away; it is better for you to lose one of your members than for your whole body to go into hell.
>
> It was also said, *"Whoever divorces his wife, let him give her a certificate of divorce."*
>
> **But I say to you** that anyone who divorces his wife, except on the ground of sexual immorality, causes her to commit adultery; and whoever marries a divorced woman commits adultery.
>
> Again, you have heard that it was said to those of ancient times, *"You shall not swear falsely, but carry out the vows you have made to the Lord."*
>
> **But I say to you:** Do not swear at all, either by heaven, for it is the throne of God, or by the earth, for it is his footstool, or by Jerusalem, for it is the city of the great King. And do not swear by your head, for you cannot make one hair white or black. Let your word be "Yes, Yes" or "No, No"; anything more than this comes from the evil one.
>
> You have heard that it was said, *"An eye for an eye and a tooth for a tooth."*
>
> **But I say to you:** Do not resist an evildoer. But if anyone strikes you on the right cheek, turn the other also, and if anyone wants to sue you and take your shirt, give your coat as well, and if anyone forces you to go one mile, go also the second mile. Give to everyone who asks of you, and do not refuse anyone who wants to borrow from you.

Finding Love

> You have heard that it was said, *"You shall love your neighbor and hate your enemy."*
> **But I say to you, Love your enemies** and pray for those who persecute you, so that you may be children of your Father in heaven, for he makes his sun rise on the evil and on the good and sends rain on the righteous and on the unrighteous. For if you love those who love you, what reward do you have? Do not even the tax-collectors do the same? And if you greet only your brothers and sisters, what more are you doing than others? Do not even the gentiles do the same? **Be perfect, therefore, as your heavenly Father is perfect.**[16]

"You shall not murder" is well known as one of the ten commandments,[17] and Jesus' warning not to be angry is the first of six reshaped commandments Jesus presents in the Sermon on the Mount. After reconfiguring, "You shall not murder," he reconfigures commandments about adultery, divorce, swearing falsely, and "an eye for an eye and tooth for a tooth" (see the table) to reach the highpoint of his reshaping of the Torah. The highpoint of Jesus' reshaping of the Torah is:

> You have heard that it was said, *"You shall love your neighbor and hate your enemy."* But I say to you: *Love your enemies* and *pray for those who persecute you*, so that you may be children of your Father in heaven, for he makes his sun rise on the evil and on the good and sends rain on the righteous and on the unrighteous. For if you love those who love you, what reward do you have? Do not even the tax-collectors do the same? And if you greet only your brothers and sisters, what more are you doing than others? Do not even the gentiles do the same? Be perfect, therefore, as your heavenly Father is perfect.[18]

We see here how Matthew's Sermon on the Mount presents reasoning and argumentation to support its reshaping of Torah. In this recitation of a commandment about love *in the Torah*, Jesus provides reasons for obeying this commandment, asks questions that lead into deep meditation on the commandment, and ends with a concluding commandment based on the nature of God. We will see in this chapter that two Jewish groups during the time of the emergence of Christianity were engaged in this kind of recitation and meditation on the commandments in the Torah. Thus, the gospel of Matthew shows us a Jesus who was an active participant alongside

---

16. Matt 5:17–48.
17. Matt 5:21; Exod 20:13; Deut 5:17; Mark 10:19; Luke 18:20.
18. Matt 5:43–48.

Loving One's Enemies as Reshaped Torah in Matthew

other Jews in updating and reshaping the Torah and the Prophets during his lifetime.

The most visible people during the time of Jesus who were engaged in a program of updating the Torah to address new dimensions of life as they arose was the Pharisees.[19] This updating of the Torah with help from the Prophets resulted in the publication of the Mishnah ca. 200 CE and the expansion of the Mishnah in both the Jerusalem Talmud and the Babylonian Talmud in subsequent centuries.[20] In Matthew Jesus joins the Pharisees in this far-reaching program of reshaping the Torah so that his followers may even *exceed the righteousness* of the Pharisees. Rather than Jesus' program in Matthew being secret, Jesus says, "Therefore every scribe who has become a disciple in the kingdom of heaven is like the master of a household who brings out of his treasure what is new and what is old."[21]

Jesus explains the relation between the old and the new in his teaching at the beginning of the Sermon on the Mount. He tells the crowds and his disciples, "Do not think that I have come to abolish the Torah or the Prophets [what is old]; I have come not to abolish but to fulfill [with what is new]."[22] After explaining that no letter will pass from the Torah until all is accomplished, he warns that whoever breaks one of the least of the commandments or teaches others to do the same "will be called least in the kingdom of heaven." But "whoever *does* them and *teaches* them will be called great in the kingdom of heaven."[23] Then he says,

> For I tell you, unless your righteousness exceeds that of the scribes and Pharisees, you will never enter the kingdom of heaven.[24]

All of this may sound confusing in the face of the assertion that many Christians make, especially citing statements from the apostle Paul, that Christians believe in faith and love rather than law. But it is important

---

19. This updating of the Torah was at first called *oral tradition* that God recited to Moses in addition to the *written tradition* (scripture). These additional traditions were gathered together in the Mishnah (ca. 200 CE); then the Mishnah was expanded with Gemara (commentary on the Mishnah) into the Jerusalem Talmud (*Yerushalmi*) by 350–400 CE and the Babylonian Talmud (*Bavli*) during 300–600 CE.

20. Scholars regularly date the Jerusalem Talmud during the fourth century CE and the Babylonian Talmud in the sixth century CE.

21. Matt 13:52–53.

22. Matt 5:17 auth. var.

23. Matt 5:19.

24. Matt 5:20.

to remember the scribe who was "near to the kingdom of God" in Mark, because he not only knew the Torah but also updated it with statements in the Prophets that make it clear that *loving* God and one's neighbor "is much more important than all whole burnt offerings and sacrifices."[25] In Matthew, Jesus openly claims to fulfill the Torah and the Prophets. His reconfiguration of six commandments in the opening chapter of the Sermon on the Mount shows a program of reshaping Torah in a manner that creates a discipline of inner spiritual guidance. In Matthew, Jesus knows that the scribes and Pharisees work diligently to live a life of righteousness according to the Torah. The challenge Jesus sets for his followers is to go even beyond the righteousness of the scribes and Pharisees with a goal of entering the kingdom of heaven. Jesus was addressing both fellow Jews who knew the Torah and people who were learning the Torah and the Prophets through his teaching.[26] His kingdom of God teaching intensifies the Torah and the Prophets with emphases present in another Jewish group we also must learn about. So let us summarize what we already know as we take one more step in our understanding.

As we know from the previous chapter on Mark, there is a strong statement about *loving God*, but there is no statement about *loving one's neighbor* in the Jewish Shema about loving God in Deuteronomy 6. *Loving one's neighbor* is a commandment in the Torah book of Leviticus (19:18), rather than in Deuteronomy, but many Jews had added the statement from Leviticus to the Shema by the first century CE. One of the possibilities for Jesus' updating of the Torah could have been to add yet another commandment in Leviticus (19:34) which says, "You shall *love the alien as yourself.*"[27] This updating would have fit well alongside a prophetic statement like Isa 1:17, which says, "Learn to do good; seek justice; rescue the oppressed; defend the orphan; plead for the widow." Instead, in Matthew Jesus begins by saying, "You have heard it said, 'You shall *love* your neighbor and *hate* your enemy.' But I say: *Love* your enemies and *pray* for those who persecute you."[28]

If we ask what group of Jews existed where someone may have heard, "*Love* your neighbor and *hate* your enemy," the answer lies in the writings

---

25. Mark 12:33–34.

26. For a book that brilliantly explores this, see John Kampen, *Matthew within Sectarian Judaism* (New Haven: Yale University Press, 2019).

27. Lev 19:34.

28. Matt 5:43–44.

of the Essenes in the Qumran Dead Sea community. We know this from discovery of new writings during the 1940s. Members of the Qumran community lived only fifteen miles east of Jerusalem alongside the Dead Sea until the destruction of their community during the Jewish-Roman Wars of 66–73 CE, and some of its members joined the early Christian movement by the time Matthew was written.[29] The *Manual of Discipline* in the Dead Sea Community says that those living according to the community covenant shall "walk *perfectly*" in God's sight by "*loving* all the children of light, each according to his lot in God's design, and *hating* all the children of darkness, each according to his guilt in God's vengeance."[30] This guideline in the Dead Sea community that gathered *in the wilderness* under the leadership of priests was designed to create a holy place where God could dwell on earth. For them, the temple in Jerusalem had become an unholy place where God could no longer dwell, because the priests there focused on wealth and riches rather than honoring God with obedience to God's covenant. For members of the Dead Sea community, priests in Jerusalem as well as "people of the land" were *children of darkness* whom they were to *hate,* while the members of the Qumran community were *children of light,* whom they were to *love*.

In Matthew's Sermon on the Mount, Jesus updates the commandment to "*love* your neighbor and *hate* your enemy," to "*Love* your enemies and *pray* for those who persecute you, *so that you may be children of your Father in heaven*."[31] For Jesus, living in special ways *in society* rather than *in a separated community* was the way to enter the kingdom of God that was drawing near. He considered *loving* enemies one encounters on a daily basis and *praying* for those who persecute you *as you live in society* to be the highest form of love commanded by God and the most complete way to fulfill the Torah and the Prophets. Jesus states this as a beatitude in the opening to the Sermon on the Mount when he says, "Blessed are the peacemakers, for *they will be called children of God*."[32] Then he adds, "Blessed are *those who are persecuted* for the sake of righteousness, for *theirs is the kingdom of heaven*."[33] To emphasize how *peacemaking love* relates to the

---

29. See Kampen, *Matthew within Sectarian Judaism*.

30. 1QS 1:9–11. Geza Vermes, *The Complete Dead Sea Scrolls in English* (New York: Penguin, 1997) 98–99.

31. Matt 5:44–45.

32. Matt 5:9.

33. Matt 5:11.

nature of God, Jesus explains that God, "makes his sun rise *on the evil and on the good* and sends rain *on the righteous and on the unrighteous*."[34] Then he asks four rhetorical questions that compare this *love* with actions of tax collectors and gentiles:

1. For if you *love* those who *love* you, what reward do you have?
2. Do not even the tax collectors do the same?
3. And if you greet only your brothers and sisters, what more are you doing than others?
4. Do not even the gentiles do the same?[35]

Questions 1 and 3 apply to us today. What reward do we have if we only love those who love us? What reward do we have if we greet only our brothers and sisters? Who is Jesus calling us to love in his teaching in the Sermon? We are called by Jesus to love people beyond those who love us, and to greet people beyond our brothers and sisters to whom we feel especially close.

After Jesus asks four rhetorical questions, he says, "Be *perfect*, therefore, as your heavenly Father is *perfect*" (Matt 5:48). While we may struggle to understand how we could possibly be *perfect*, this commandment by Jesus resonates fully with the statement about *walking perfectly* in God's sight in the Manual of Discipline of the Dead Sea Community. While members of the Dead Sea Community *walked perfectly* by loving according to *priestly* guidelines in the Torah, for Jesus *loving* one's enemies even when one is persecuted for friendship with tax collectors and gentiles is the way of *walking perfectly* in God's sight. In other words, here Jesus moves beyond guidelines for living *within a holy community* by applying the Torah and Prophets to the challenges of living *a daily life in society* where you are ridiculed for your manner of loving and caring for others.

I have to admit that I have significant discomfort with the concept of perfection. But Jesus uses this word, as did also the Essenes at Qumran, to explain the challenge before us. Much of my early training in life held perfection as the goal for my actions. I was taught to feel guilty, or at least ashamed, if I did not lead a perfect life. But what does perfection mean? Can any of us really do anything *perfectly*? I remember when I was around ten or eleven years old I tried to play pieces of music on the piano absolutely perfectly. I vividly recall a noontime when, after we had eaten what

34. Matt 5:45.
35. Matt 5:46–47.

we called dinner, I played the piece of music for our family that I would soon be playing at a piano recital. I played all of it perfectly, from my point of view, except for one note where I hesitated a bit before I played it. When I completed the piece, my father said, "I am sure you will work on that one place where you didn't quite get it right." He offered no compliment for the way I had played the rest of the piece! Nothing more. What I heard was, "You didn't play it *perfectly* yet, *did* you?" Perhaps this is why I finally gave up trying to play the piano better later in my life, even after I had a couple of years of piano lessons in college. It was only when I found a wife who helped me understand that none of us is perfect, that I began to accept my imperfections. This has helped me attain much higher goals than I ever could have believed as a child that I could ever attain.

So what does it mean to be *perfect* in the eyes of God? Perhaps the highest point of *perfection* Jesus sets forth in the gospel of Matthew actually occurs in Matt 25:31–46 when people, *without knowing it,* gave *the least of these* food when they were hungry, water when they were thirsty, hospitality when they were a stranger, clothing when they were naked, and visited them when they were in prison. The *perfection* is that these people *did not even know what they did* so they were judged by the Son of man to be *righteous.* So, what is *perfection* in the eyes of God?

I think it helps us to know that the Greek word translated as *perfect* in the New Testament is *teleios,* which is related to *telos,* meaning *end* or *final.* As an adjective, *teleios* means *mature, complete,* or *finished.* God is *fully developed, mature, and complete* both in the view of the leaders of the Dead Sea community and of Jesus in Matthew. For Jesus and for members of the community, *fulfilling* the Torah and the Prophets requires *walking* in a *fully developed, mature, and complete* way with God. When Jesus says he has come "to fulfill the Torah and the Prophets,"[36] he means he has come to clarify how it is possible to live among tax collectors and gentiles, rather than to be separated from society like members of the Dead Sea community lived. For Jesus, *loving one's enemies* and *praying for those who persecute you* is the way truly to fulfill all the commandments (613 according to later rabbis) in the Torah and to live according to the teachings of the Prophets whom God called to guide the people of Israel in obedience to the Torah.

For Jesus in the gospel of Matthew, therefore, *loving one's enemies* is the fullest, most mature form of love. This reminds us of Paul's statement at the end of his famous chapter thirteen of 1 Corinthians on love that when

36. Matt 5:17.

he was a child he spoke like a child, thought like a child, and reasoned like a child, but when he became an adult he put an end to childish ways.[37] But Jesus is saying even more than this in the gospel of Matthew. He is saying, "Put an end to childish ways so fully that you can even *love* your enemies."

So who are the tax collectors and gentiles in our own midst? Tax collectors at the time of Jesus were Jews who collected taxes for Rome. They regularly *bought the rights* from Roman officials to collect taxes in a particular district. Whatever additional money they could collect was their own income. This arrangement led to widespread abuse as many tax collectors collected larger sums than they should have through maneuvering and threats to their fellow Jews. So a direct parallel to our time would be defrauders and scammers. And who are the gentiles in our midst? I suppose they are people whom we perceive not to live a moral and caring mode of life.

I think another way to approach this, if we follow the spirit of Matthew's presentation of Jesus, is to think about how we must update Matthew for our own time. Are our most difficult enemies today people who hold political views that oppose our views? Are they members of *another* political party? This has become very difficult in our recent time, causing significant problems even within families, especially during special times of gathering like Thanksgiving, Christmas, and Easter. Here we can benefit from a group like *Braver Angels of Georgia*, where leaders work with local communities by holding workshops, debates, and public presentations designed to bridge the political divide we experience in our country.[38]

A special aspect of Jesus' teaching in the Sermon on the Mount is his teaching of the Lord's prayer soon after his teaching to *love* one's enemies and *pray* for those who persecute us. In this version of the Lord's prayer, Jesus especially emphasizes *forgiving* others. After praying, "And forgive us our debts, as we also have forgiven our debtors," Jesus says:

> For if you forgive others their trespasses, your heavenly Father will also forgive you, but if you do not forgive others, neither will your Father forgive your trespasses.[39]

---

37. 1 Cor 13:11.
38. https://georgia.braverangels.org/about-us.
39. Matt 6:14–15.

Loving One's Enemies as Reshaped Torah in Matthew

For Jesus, in the gospel of Matthew, *praying* for those who persecute us and *forgiving* others their trespasses against us is a way of living in the *perfection of* God.

In the back of my mind I keep hearing the story about Abraham Lincoln when a woman rebuked him for his lenient attitude toward the South. In response to her feeling that the South should be "destroyed" after the Civil War, he replied, "Madam, do I not destroy my enemies when I make them my friends?"[40] This seems to me to be a truly *adult* way to approach our problem of having enemies. The problem, of course, is that many of our enemies do not exist in the space where we live so we could try to make them our friends. Is Jesus, therefore, challenging us to change our *feelings* so we do not nurture *attitudes* of hatred? This seems to take us beyond *making* enemies or *seeing* people as enemies toward transforming ourselves into people who *change our predispositions* through *disciplined practices* of love and empathy. Our love will then include *all* people, *including* people toward whom we almost automatically feel hatred. This indeed is a difficult standard, but we must work daily toward this goal, even when the goal itself seems impossible.

There is one more place in Matthew where Jesus speaks of *perfection*, and we will close this chapter with a discussion of this story. Jesus' program for reshaping the Torah continues into Matthew's presentation of Jesus' response to the rich man who comes to him asking what he must do to have eternal life. When Jesus recites the commandments the man must keep to have eternal life, after saying, "Also, you shall *love* your neighbor as yourself,"[41] he adds, "If you wish to be *perfect*, go, sell your possessions, give the money to the poor, and you will have treasure in heaven; then come, follow me."[42] An interesting thing here is that the members of the Dead Sea community brought all their possessions and money and gave them to the community for its treasury and supplies. In Matthew, the rich man can walk in *perfection* by selling his possessions, giving them to the poor, and following Jesus. The challenge is to live a life of *perfection* even as one is persecuted in a society occupied by tax collectors and gentiles. This life of *perfection* shows the way toward inheriting eternal life.

---

40. https://rb.gy/56ug6.
41. Matt 19:19.
42. Matt 19:21.

In addition to expanding Mark's version of the story of the rich man, Matthew expands Jesus' response to his disciples by referring to the end time. Jesus says to them,

> "Truly I tell you, *at the renewal of all things, when the Son of Man is seated on the throne of his glory, you who have followed me will also sit on twelve thrones, judging the twelve tribes of Israel*. And everyone who has left houses or brothers or sisters or father or mother or children or fields, for my name's sake will receive a hundredfold, and will inherit eternal life. But many who are first will be last, and the last will be first."[43]

The Matthean addition about the Son of Man to Jesus' teaching reminds us of Matthew 25:31–46, where the Son of Man comes and separates the righteous from the unrighteous like sheep and goats, and the unrighteous "go away into eternal punishment *but the righteous into eternal life*."[44] There is no talk in Matthew 25 of Jesus' disciples "sit[ting] on twelve thrones, judging the twelve tribes of Israel."[45] Rather, the Son of Man comes as a King who judges *people of all the nations*. For our purposes, it is important to observe that the focus in Matthew is on *righteousness* as a way to inherit eternal life. Indeed, righteousness is *the way* to "be *perfect* as your heavenly Father is *perfect*" and to inherit eternal life in Matthew.

CONCLUSION

During this phase of our journey we have seen the expansion of *love* in Matthew to include *loving* one's enemies and *praying* for those who persecute us. Jesus presents this as a commandment in the Sermon on the Mount that establishes an environment for Jesus' discussion of being "*perfect* as your heavenly Father is *perfect*." Then, when the rich man comes to Jesus in Matthew asking how he can have eternal life, Jesus rehearses commandments to him, then tells him that if he wishes to be *perfect*, he must sell his possessions, give money to the poor, and come, follow him.

This phase of our journey has shown us how God's love comes into the world on the wings of the Torah and the Prophets in Matthew. This love extends *even* to *enemies*, who seem primarily to be tax collectors and

---

43. Matt 19:28–30.
44. Matt 25:46.
45. Matt 19:28.

gentiles in this gospel. Is the message in Matthew that we must go out of our way to *love* people who are despised and mistrusted by others and even by ourselves? It would seem so.

In conclusion, Matthew rewrites Mark's stories to show Jesus teaching *new Torah*. Matthew is clearly interested in people *living a life of love*. Matthew's gospel shows this new way by updating the Torah and the Prophets as it presents a gospel of the life, death, and resurrection of Jesus. For Matthew, living a life of *righteousness* includes *loving* even one's enemies. This way of life enacts a full, complete, *perfect* form of love in the world.

The gospel of Luke, to which we turn next, also presents Jesus teaching that we must *love our enemies*. Somewhat different emphases, however, create the framework and the context of this love in Luke's gospel. Let us turn to Luke's significantly different way of rewriting Mark's gospel to show love as *a way of life* in relation to Jesus who has come as God's Messiah to the world.

QUESTIONS FOR DISCUSSION

1. In your view, why would the gospel of Matthew have the divine voice tell John the Baptist, "This is my Son, the Beloved (*agapētos*), with whom I am well pleased"? Notice that the divine voice does not say, "Listen to him," like the divine voice says to the disciples in the Transfiguration.

2. Do you agree that the Sermon on the Mount in the gospel of Matthew shows Jesus as a *new Moses* who *reshapes* the teaching that God gave to Moses on Mount Sinai? If so, what is the significance of this for early Christianity? What is the significance of this for Christianity today?

3. Why do you think the Sermon on the Mount in Matthew presents Jesus as gradually reshaping Torah from "Love your neighbor as yourself," which is in Lev 19:18, to "Love your enemies and pray for those who persecute you" (Matt 5:44)?

4. What do you think is the relation of Jesus' teaching to "Love your enemies and pray for those who persecute you" to his statement that "unless your righteousness exceeds that of the scribes and Pharisees, you will never enter the kingdom of heaven" (Matt 5:20)?

5. On the basis of information provided in the discussion of the gospel of Matthew in this chapter, who do you think were the *enemies* when Jesus tells the crowd to love their enemies? Who are your *enemies* today whom Jesus' message challenges you to love?

6. When Jesus teaches, "Be perfect as your heavenly Father is perfect" (Matt 5:48), what kind of *perfection* do you think Jesus means? Are there different ways to understand *perfection*? Do you think there was a different way of understanding perfection when Jesus lived than how we understand perfection today? If so, what may be the differences and why?

7. Why do you think Jesus challenged the rich man to be *perfect* by selling his possessions, giving the money to the poor, and coming to follow him as a disciple? Can we follow Jesus as disciples if we do not sell all our possessions and give the money to the poor? Is it simply impossible for us to fulfill what Jesus requires in this story? Or is there a way we can appropriately revise what Jesus says here and still fulfill what Jesus is asking in this story?

3

Loving One's Enemies as Prophetic Wisdom in Luke

> Jesus said, "But I say to you who are listening: Love your enemies; do good to those who hate you."[1]

IN THE FIRST CHAPTER we found God's love hiding in the mystery and confusion of the coming of the kingdom of God in Mark. This love remains significantly hidden in Jesus' activity of calling disciples, healing people, suffering, dying, and rising. In the second chapter we saw God's love coming into the world on the wings of the Torah and the Prophets. In Matthew, Jesus teaches like the Pharisees teach, updating and reshaping the Torah and the Prophets on the basis of new challenges God's people face. Also, Jesus focuses on living a life devoted to the perfection of God in Matthew. In this present chapter we see God's love coming into the world through Jesus' prophetic blessing of the poor and marginalized, and his announcement of the burden of wealth for those who respond to the coming of God's kingdom. Jesus' prophetic teaching in Luke shows a pathway forward by loving one's enemies, praying for those who persecute them, and by giving without expecting anything in return.

The gospel of Luke brings to mind a special uncle, a brother of my father. As I was growing up on a farm in Nebraska, my parents were

---

1. Luke 6:27.

continually in debt. My parents were tenant farmers on land owned by my grandfather. Since my grandfather who would not sell the farm to my parents, there was no way for my father and mother to improve their basic economic situation. They were always indebted to my grandfather. My father was the oldest of three boys. He wanted to go to college, so he started at a church college in Iowa after high school. My grandfather, however, bought a new farm and told him he had to come home and help him run the new farm. The next oldest son, my uncle, completed college, received a teaching degree, and started teaching at various grade schools. Within time he focused on teaching music, got a teaching position in Ohio, and moved to a large city in Ohio. After my older brother was allowed to spend the summer with this favorite uncle when he was fourteen years of age, my younger brother and I also were allowed to spend the summer in this large city with my uncle and his wife and children when we were fourteen years of age.

I have always had a special place in my heart for this favorite uncle. In contrast to my father, he was able to buy some houses and rent them out to add to his income. He was very thrifty, but he was also generous. Every summer he would take a vacation drive to visit relatives in Nebraska. The trunk of his car was always packed full, and we knew he had special gifts for us somewhere in that trunk so full of things. When my father needed additional money beyond what he could get as a loan at the local bank, my uncle would loan him money. When my father paid it back, my uncle would never accept interest on the money he loaned to him.

After I went through graduate school and started teaching at the University of Illinois at Urbana-Champaign, I was granted a Fulbright Fellowship a year after I had taken a sabbatical. I wanted to take the Fellowship, but I had to take a leave without pay to accept it. My uncle loaned me and my wife $3,000 so we could pay basic expenses that allowed us to move to Norway for a year as a Fulbright Professor at the University of Trondheim. During the year abroad I accepted a new teaching position at Emory University in Atlanta, Georgia, and spent the rest of my teaching career there. After we moved to Atlanta and I was talking with my uncle on the phone, he asked me what it was like living in a communist country for a year. I was taken aback and asked him what he meant. He said, "Well they have socialized medicine in Norway, don't they?" I said, "Yes, but Norway is a Lutheran nation, and I was sponsored by a Methodist professor." As I continued by telling him many graduate students in Norway are members of the Salvation Army, I realized I was dealing with many complex issues in the context of my deep love of my uncle.

In this chapter we will wrestle with the *complexity* of God's friendship with us in relation to the complexities of our friendship and love of others. In other words, we will notice that Scripture talks about the topic of love in many different ways, because Scripture is becoming God's wisdom during the time of Jesus. Each writing in the New Testament has its own way of talking about love, even though there is much overlap. As we continue our journey we will ask why each writer wrote in the way he did. Often we are not able to answer the question as fully as we might like, but we will shed as much light on the context of the writer as is feasible in this short book.

From the standpoint of biblical theology, Stephen Fowl argues that the multiple ways scripture approaches topics creates an environment where believers may deepen their knowledge and friendship with God. In Fowl's words:

> Because God loves humans and desires to draw us into an ever-deeper friendship, God, through the Spirit, breathes a multiplicity of meanings into scripture. In this way, God invites believers to deepen their knowledge of and friendship with God through repeated and ongoing engagement with scripture.[2]

In this chapter we will follow the way Luke presents Jesus teaching that we should love our enemies. On this journey, we will remind ourselves that Stephen Fowl says differences in Scripture are *a good thing*. The different ways in which Jesus describes God, and the different episodes in which Jesus speaks and acts, show us different aspects of *loving God, loving our neighbors as ourselves,* and *loving our enemies* that can inform us in our daily lives.

LOVING ONE'S ENEMIES IN LUKE'S SERMON ON THE PLAIN

Instead of a Sermon on the Mount, as in Matt 5–7, Luke has a Sermon on the Plain.[3] This sermon is like Moses' teaching of the Israelites in Deuteronomy,

---

2. Stephen Fowl, "Christian Theological Interpretation," in *The New Cambridge Companion to Biblical Interpretation*, ed. Ian Boxall and Bradley C. Gregory (Cambridge: Cambridge University Press, 2023) 183 [173–90].

3. Luke 6:17–49.

the last book of the Torah, rather than being like his teaching in Exodus at Mount Sinai. Deuteronomy begins with, "These are the words that Moses spoke to all Israel beyond the Jordan—in the wilderness, *on the plain* opposite Suph, between Paran and Tophel, Laban, Hazeroth, and Di-zahab."[4] Moses speaks on this level plain in the wilderness to prepare the Israelites for their travel to the land of Canaan/Israel as their final destination. As Moses speaks in Deuteronomy, he updates the previous commandments of God with guidelines for what they must do to keep their hearts, eyes, minds, and bodies *on God* when they reach the land of milk, honey, silver, and gold in the land of Canaan (modern day Israel). The problem is that when they reach the rich and bountiful land, they will focus on *what they themselves have achieved* rather than on *how God has blessed them* in this new location.

After the first five chapters of Deuteronomy, Moses recites to the Israelites the Shema, which we have discussed earlier in the chapter on Mark. The Shema reiterates the necessity for them, above all, to *love* the Lord God with all their heart, and with all their soul, and with all their might.[5] After explaining to the Israelites all the things they must do to *keep their eyes and hearts on God* while they are in the land of Canaan, Moses presents *blessings and curses* to them in Deuteronomy 28. In summary, the blessings say that if they obey the Lord their God by diligently observing all his commandments, *blessed* shall they be in the city and the field; the fruit of their womb, the ground, and their livestock; their basket and kneading bowl; when they come in and when they go out.[6] In contrast, if they do not obey the Lord God, *cursed* shall they be in the city and the field; their basket and kneading bowl; the fruit of their womb, the ground, and their livestock.[7] The *blessings and curses* toward the end of Deuteronomy show how *living a life of loving God* will bring blessing, and how *a life of turning away from God* will bring curses.

Luke's Sermon on the Plain, which is a reshaping of Moses' teaching in Deuteronomy, begins with *blessings and woes* that set the stage for Jesus' teaching on *loving as a way of life*. In Luke, Jesus reshapes Moses' *blessings* and *curses* in Deuteronomy into *blessings* and *woes*. The focus of the blessings (beatitudes) is on the poor and marginalized:

---

4. Deut 1:1.
5. Deut 6:5.
6. Deut 28:1–6.
7. Deut 28:15–19.

Loving One's Enemies as Prophetic Wisdom in Luke

> Blessed are you who are poor,
> > for yours is the kingdom of God.
>
> Blessed are you who are hungry now,
> > for you will be filled.
>
> Blessed are you who weep now,
> > for you will laugh.
>
> Blessed are you when people hate you,
> > and when they exclude you, revile you,
> > and defame you on account of the Son of Man.
>
> Rejoice on that day and leap for joy,
> > for surely your reward is great in heaven,
> > for that is how their ancestors treated the prophets.[8]

In Luke, Jesus does not say, "Blessed are the *poor in spirit*," as in Matthew 5:3, but, "Blessed are *you who are poor*." In Luke, Jesus is addressing people who *really are poor*. Also, he does not speak *about* the poor as a topic, but he speaks directly *to* them. In Luke, then, the *poor* are *in the crowd* to whom Jesus is speaking! This focus on the poor is directly related to Jesus' emphasis as he started his adult ministry in his hometown of Nazareth. When he went to his hometown synagogue on the sabbath, and the scroll of Isaiah the prophet was given to him to read, it started with,

> The Spirit of the Lord is upon me,
> > because he has anointed me
> > to bring good news (gospel) to the poor.[9]

For Jesus in Luke, the poor *in his midst* are a major focus. The *gospel* Jesus preaches is *good news* to *the poor*. This emphasis comes especially from *the Prophets* rather than *the Torah*. As a result, Jesus adopts a *prophetic tone* as he speaks. In the same context where he speaks prophetic blessing on the marginalized and needy, he adopts a tone of *severe criticism* of the wealthy who live in luxury and do not share their wealth with the needy. Thus, in Luke Jesus moves directly from his beatitudes to the poor to *woes* to the rich:

> But woe to you who are rich,
> > for you have received your consolation.
>
> Woe to you who are full now,
> > for you will be hungry.
>
> Woe to you who are laughing now,
> > for you will mourn and weep.

8. Luke 6:20–23.
9. Luke 4:18.

> Woe to you when all speak well of you,
>> for that is how their ancestors treated the false prophets.[10]

Jesus does not speak *about* the wealthy, but directly *to* them. In other words, both rich people and poor people are in the crowd to whom he is speaking. This is directly related to Moses' teaching in the book of Deuteronomy about the necessity of the people of Israel to share the riches from *the land of milk and honey,* namely Canaan/Israel, with the poor, the widow, and the alien *in their midst*. And this emphasis was especially taken up by the Prophets who criticized Israel's leaders for focusing on rituals without also focusing on the needs of the poor, marginalized, and underprivileged. Thus, the opening chapter of the book of Isaiah, the writing Jesus read aloud in the synagogue at Nazareth, starts with one of the famous criticisms of focusing only on temple rituals:

> What to me is the multitude of your sacrifices?
>> says YHWH;
>
> I have had enough of burnt offerings of rams
>> and the fat of fed beasts;
>
> I do not delight in the blood of bulls
>> or of lambs or of goats.[11]

And this criticism leads a few verses later to:

> Wash yourselves; make yourselves clean;
>> remove your evil deeds from before my eyes;
>
> cease to do evil;
>> learn to do good;
>
> seek justice;
>> rescue the oppressed;
>
> defend the orphan;
>> plead for the widow.[12]

In the context of the prophetic emphasis on caring for the poor, the orphan, and the widow, the Greek Old Testament version of Isaiah uses the verb *to proclaim the gospel* (*euangelizomai*) six times. The first two occurrences are in the chapter where *a voice* cries out to Israel, "In the wilderness prepare

---

10. Luke 6:24–26.
11. Isa 1:11 auth. var.
12. Isa 1:16–17.

the way of the LORD,"[13] which is applied to John the Baptist in the gospels.[14] A few verses later in Isaiah *a voice* says:

> Get you up to a high mountain,
>   O Zion, herald of the gospel (*euangelizomenos*);
> lift up your voice with strength,
>   O Jerusalem, herald of the gospel (*euangelizomenos*),
>   lift it up, do not fear;
> say to the cities of Judah,
>   "Here is your God!"[15]

The next two occurrences emerge as YHWH speaks out in Isaiah 52:

> How beautiful upon the mountains
>   are the feet of the messenger who preaches the
> gospel (*euangelizomenou*) of peace,
> who brings the gospel (*euangelizomenos*),
>   who announces salvation,
> who says to Zion, 'Your God reigns.'[16]

The fifth occurrence in Isaiah 60:6, which the reader will see as related to the story of the magi in the birth of Jesus in Matthew says:

> A multitude of camels shall cover you,
>   the young camels of Midian and Ephah;
>   all those from Sheba shall come.
>
> They shall bring gold and frankincense[17]
>   and shall proclaim the gospel (*euangeliountai*) of the salvation
>   of YHWH.

The sixth occurrence is in the chapter that provides the words for the opening of Jesus' reading from Isaiah in the Nazareth synagogue:

> The spirit of YHWH God is upon me,
>   because YHWH has anointed me;
>   he has sent me to proclaim the gospel (*euangelisasthai*) to the
>   poor.[18]

---

13. Isa 40:3.
14. Mark 1:3; Matt 3:3; Luke 3:4; John 1:23.
15. Isa 40:9 LXX auth. trans.
16. Isa 52:7 LXX auth. trans.
17. Isa 60:6 LXX auth. trans.; Matt 2:11.
18. Isa 61:1 LXX auth. trans.

The emphasis on proclaiming the gospel (*euangelizesthai*) in the prophetic book of Isaiah is important for understanding the gospel of Luke. In Luke, rather than *reshaping Torah*, Jesus embodies the continuation of *prophetic proclamation of the gospel of God* in Isaiah, which includes criticism of the wealthy who do not share their riches with the poor, needy, and marginalized.

Thus, in Luke's Sermon on the Plain, Jesus' program is not *reshaping the Torah* but *speaking prophetic wisdom* to *all people*. Jesus *embodies* the spirit of the prophet Isaiah as he speaks *to* the poor and *to* the wealthy. This leads directly to the reason Jesus teaches about *loving enemies* in the Sermon on the Plain. Immediately after the *blessings and woes* at the beginning of the Sermon on the Plain, Jesus introduces *love* as the primary topic of his prophetic sermon:

> But I say to you who are listening:
> *Love* your enemies;
>   do good to those who hate you;
>   bless those who curse you;
>   pray for those who mistreat you.[19]

In Luke's Sermon on the Plain there is no gradual *working* through a series of commandments to a climax in "*Love* your enemies," as in Matthew. Rather, in Luke Jesus transforms Torah teaching into prophetic wisdom that teaches *loving one's enemies* as internal to a *prophetic life*. Anyone who lives a prophetic life of God's wisdom about caring for the poor and marginalized knows that prophets are not *loved* by those who have wealth and power. Thus, Jesus says,

> Woe to you when all speak well of you,
>   for that is how their ancestors treated the false prophets.[20]

People do not speak well of true prophets. People only speak well of *false prophets*. True prophets are spoken against and abused, because they speak words from God that deeply challenge the rich and powerful. Jesus wants his followers to know that if all people speak well of them they are not speaking in a prophetic voice that calls on the wealthy and powerful to help those who are poor and marginalized.

---

19. Luke 6:27–28.
20. Luke 6:26.

Matthew's Sermon on the Mount[21]	Luke's Sermon on the Plain[22]
(Reshaping of Torah)	(Transformation into Prophetic Wisdom)
For I tell you, unless your righteousness exceeds that of the scribes and Pharisees, you will never enter the kingdom of heaven.	Woe to you when all speak well of you, for that is how their ancestors treated the false prophets.
You have heard that it was said to those of ancient times, "*You shall not murder,*" and "*whoever murders shall be liable to judgment.*" **But I say to you** . . . You have heard that it was said, "*You shall not commit adultery.*" **But I say to you** . . . It was also said, "*Whoever divorces his wife, let him give her a certificate of divorce.*" **But I say to you** . . . Again, you have heard that it was said to those of ancient times, "*You shall not swear falsely, but carry out the vows you have made to the Lord.*" **But I say to you** . . . You have heard that it was said, "*An eye for an eye and a tooth for a tooth.*" **But I say to you**. . . You have heard that it was said, "*You shall love your neighbor and hate your enemy.*" **But I say to you,**	**But I say to you** who are listening:
Love your enemies and pray for those who persecute you, so that you may be children of your Father in heaven,	**Love your enemies;** do good to those who hate you; bless those who curse you; pray for those who mistreat you.
for he makes his sun rise on the evil and on the good and sends rain on the righteous and on the unrighteous.	If anyone strikes you on the cheek, offer the other also; and from anyone who takes away your coat do not withhold even your shirt.

21. Matt 5:20–22, 27–28, 31–34, 38–39, 43–48.
22. Luke 6:26–36.

	Give to everyone who asks of you,
	and if anyone takes away what is yours, do not ask for it back again.
	Do to others as you would have them do to you.
For if you love those who love you, what reward do you have? Do not even the tax-collectors do the same?	**If you love those who love you,** what credit is that to you? For even sinners love those who love them.
And if you greet only your brothers and sisters, what more are you doing than others? Do not even the gentiles do the same?	If you do good to those who do good to you, what credit is that to you? For even sinners do the same.
	If you lend to those from whom you expect to receive payment, what credit is that to you? Even sinners lend to sinners, to receive as much again.
	Instead, love your enemies, do good, and lend, expecting nothing in return.
	Your reward will be great, and you will be children of the Most High; for he himself is kind to the ungrateful and the wicked.
Be perfect, therefore, as your heavenly Father is perfect.	**Be merciful**, just as your Father is merciful.

Perhaps we need to step back a moment to take a breath and try to absorb this very difficult teaching. Most of us who are reading what the prophetic book of Isaiah says, and what Jesus says in Luke, are challenged by the fact that we are not poor, needy, and marginalized. We have abundant food, clothing, and housing. Thus, when it comes to *loving our enemies*, perhaps *our perceived enemies* are those who want to take our wealth *from us* and give it to the poor, needy, and marginalized. But we also know that *those who give* are regularly *much loved*. My *beloved uncle* regularly gave us good things when we lived on the farm. Then when we went to stay with him the summer we were fourteen years of age, he gave us money for working for him. When I started college, he gave me a *Webster's Collegiate Dictionary*, which I have to this day. Then when I was in seminary in the city where he lived, he and his wife not only regularly invited us to delicious Sunday dinners in their home, but he hired me during the summers to help him repair and refurbish properties he rented out to couples and families. My family and I were blessed by the generosity of my uncle. He exists as a model for me as I face the responsibility of sharing my privileged status with those who are marginalized and needy. But what about *enemies*?

In Luke, while one's neighbor is *one who is near,* one's enemy is *one who is against* in one's own community. When Jesus opened his ministry in his hometown synagogue in Nazareth by reading from Isaiah about his good news to the poor, those to whom he read turned against him. They became angry at him, because he emphasized how Elijah had not been sent to widows in Israel but to a widow at Zarephath in Sidon, which is Gentile territory. Then Jesus says that Elisha was not sent to heal lepers in Israel but to Namaan the Syrian, another Gentile.[23] For Jesus in Luke, then, Prophets did not speak out simply to Israelites, but to *all people*. At this point, the people in the synagogue at Nazareth "were filled with rage." They wanted to throw him off a cliff, but he escaped.[24] In the context of this anger against him, to which Jesus responded with, "No prophet is accepted in his hometown," Jesus went to Capernaum and continued his ministry in the synagogue there by healing a man with an unclean demon.[25] Thus, while many people turned against Jesus at the very beginning of his ministry, he did not turn away from people who needed to be healed and to hear his message of "good news to the poor" and "recovery of sight to the blind."[26]

We have seen in previous chapters that many Jews already joined *loving God* with *loving one's neighbor* by the time of Jesus. We have also seen how members of the Dead Sea Community had said to *love* the children of light and *hate* the children of darkness. In Luke's Sermon on the Plain, Jesus continues the prophetic ministry he started at Nazareth by focusing first and foremost on the poor and the wealthy. But then he turns immediately to *loving one's enemies* after introducing the Sermon on the Plain with *blessings and woes.* After announcing the topic of *loving one's enemies,* Jesus describes two *situations in life* that call for *straightforward exhibiting of love* in one's relation to people who abuse them: "If anyone strikes you on the cheek, offer the other also, and from anyone who takes away your coat do

23. Luke 4:25–27.
24. Luke 4:28–30.
25. Luke 4:31–37.
26. Luke 4:18.

Finding Love

not withhold even your shirt."[27] Then Jesus focuses on people *in need* as well as people who abuse them: "Give to everyone who asks of you; and if anyone takes away what is yours, do not ask for it back again."[28] Then Jesus presents a statement that summarizes this *introductory part* of the Sermon on the Plain: "Do to others as you would have them do to you."[29]

If we think Jesus has now completed his teaching on *love*, we are incorrect. Jesus has introduced *love* as *a way of life* with other people to reach the highpoint of *thinking about others as though they were ourselves*. Love is caring for people even when they hate you. It is also caring for others even when some complain about your caring for those who are needy and marginalized. After Jesus makes his summary statement, "*Do to others as you would have them do to you,*" he is ready to take the second step, where he addresses *the nature of our love for others*.

To get us to think more deeply about the nature of our love, Jesus asks three *rhetorical questions*. A *rhetorical question* is a question to which the hearer knows the answer. In this instance, we know to answer, "No thanks at all."[30] Jesus presupposes all will know the correct answer, so he supplements each answer with a statement that even *sinners* do this.

1. If you *love* those who *love* you, what thanks do you get for it? [No thanks at all.] For even sinners *love* those who *love* them.

2. If you do good to those who do good to you, what thanks do you get for it? [No thanks at all.] For even sinners do the same.

3. If you lend to those from whom you expect to receive payment, what thanks do you get for it? [No thanks at all.] Even sinners lend to sinners, to receive as much again.[31]

With each question, Jesus drives deeper down into the nature of our love for others. Do we only love those who love us? Do we only do good to those who do good to us? Do we only lend to others when we expect something in return? Ouch! Ouch! Ouch! Perhaps we do! But, Jesus says, we must move beyond this to love even those who do *not* love us. We must do good even to those who do *evil* against us. We must *give*, expecting nothing in

---

27. Luke 6:29.
28. Luke 6:30.
29. Luke 6:31.
30. The Greek word here is *charis*, which in this context means *thanks* or *gratitude* rather than *grace*.
31. Luke 6:32–34 auth. var.

return. Where can we find the inner spiritual resources for acting in this *loving manner*? The answer for Jesus lies in the nature of *God's love*. Therefore, Jesus builds a crescendo to God's love in the final part of his teaching about loving one's enemies.

Jesus starts with a summary of what he has taught: "Instead, *love* your enemies, do good, and lend, expecting nothing in return."[32] Then he turns to the *divine passive* part: "Your reward will be great, and you will be children of the Most High; for he himself is kind to the ungrateful and the wicked."[33] The *active meaning* of this is: "*God* will reward you greatly; *God* will make you children of the Most High; for *God* is kind to the ungrateful and the wicked." Then Jesus ends with a *conclusion* that calls people to action: "Be *merciful*, just as your Father is *merciful*."[34] Now Jesus has us where he wants us, namely in a place where we see and understand the nature of God's mercy. A side note here is that in the Qur'an *God's mercy* is without limit, but that is another story for another time. To see how Jesus develops this understanding with a story, we turn to the parable of the Good Samaritan in Luke.

JESUS TELLS ABOUT AN *ENEMY WHO IS A MERCIFUL NEIGHBOR* IN LUKE

Having started with *loving your enemies* as a *way of life* in the Sermon on the Plain in Luke 6, we now turn to Jesus' parable on *loving one's neighbor* as a *way of life* in Luke 10. In this section we want to ask if Luke's changing of the discussion of *love of one's enemy* to *love of one's neighbor* may be grounded in an insight that *perceiving of someone as our enemy* is actually an *inner process* of creating enemies *within our own heart* as a *habit of the heart and mind*. The man the Samaritan finds in the ditch in the parable we are about to discuss is *not* a person who can *hurt* the Samaritan walking on the road from Jerusalem to Jericho. Isn't an *enemy* someone who can physically harm another person? Fortunately, most of us do not live in environments where we are continually in danger from others. This may be different from the environments in which the gospels of Matthew and Luke were written. But even in their environments, the stories they know about Jesus exhibited a *love of enemies* in such a way that they also perceive Jesus

---

32. Luke 6:35a.
33. Luke 6:35bc.
34. Luke 6:36.

to have *taught* that one should love their enemies. Could this be because people then and now regularly *create enemies in their hearts and minds* simply as a matter of habit?

In Luke 10:1–16 Jesus sends seventy-two followers out ahead of him "to every town and place where he himself intended to go" (10:1), and he explains to them that he is sending them out "like lambs into the midst of wolves" (10:3). When they return with joy, Jesus rejoices in the Holy Spirit, expresses thanksgiving to his Father, and blesses the disciples for seeing what they see and hearing what they hear (10:17–24). At this point, a lawyer *stands up* and tests Jesus by asking him what he must do to inherit *eternal life*. Jesus asks him, "What is written in the Torah? What do you read there?"[35] We have noticed how Jesus started his ministry by going to Nazareth and *reading* from the prophetic book of Isaiah in his home synagogue on the Sabbath.[36] Here we see Jesus engage the lawyer with *what is written in the Torah*. We also see what Jesus understands as *walking* in the way of life *of the Torah*. When the lawyer responds to Jesus, the lawyer does not recite the Shema, but immediately joins the statement about *loving* the Lord your God with *loving* one's neighbor as oneself.[37] Without delay, Jesus says to him, "You have given the right answer; *do this, and you will live.*" For Jesus, the answer lies in *doing* rather than simply in *saying*. But then the man asks Jesus, "And who is *my neighbor*?"[38]

At this point, Jesus tells the man the parable of the Good Samaritan. To understand this parable, it is important for us to know what happened in the preceding chapter in Luke. In Luke 9:51 Jesus "set his face to go to Jerusalem." When some of Jesus' disciples enter a village of the Samaritans to prepare for Jesus' coming there, the Samaritans will not receive Jesus, "because his face was set toward Jerusalem."[39] At this point James and John

---

35. Luke 10:26 auth. var.
36. Luke 4:16–20.
37. Luke 10:27.
38. Luke 10:28–29.
39. Luke 9:52–53. Samaritans were Israelites who remained in Israel when the Jerusalem temple was destroyed and Judean leaders were taken into exile in Babylonia. Samaritans worshipped on Mt. Gerizim near Nablus after the Jerusalem temple was destroyed. By Jesus' time they were considered ethnically and religiously different from Jews (*Ioudaioi*) because they had intermarried with people in the area rather than only with the Judean population. Samaritans regularly would not help people traveling to Jerusalem for a festival, because they considered them to be going to the wrong sanctuary. They should be going to Mount Gerizim to worship God.

Loving One's Enemies as Prophetic Wisdom in Luke

ask Jesus whether they should "command fire to come down from heaven and consume them."[40] It is quite clear that James and John perceive these Samaritans to be their enemies, and they wonder if they should call the vengeance of God down on them to consume them, like Elijah had called down fire from heaven on hostile troops.[41] When Jesus turns and rebukes them for saying this,[42] he is enacting the command to "love one's enemies," which he teaches in the Sermon on the Plain. But then he goes even further in Luke 10 when he features a Samaritan as *the good neighbor* to a wounded man in the ditch.

In order to get the full import of this, let us remember not only Jesus' statement in the Sermon on the Plain, "Love your enemies, do good to those who hate you," but also "Be merciful as your heavenly Father is merciful."[43] Isn't Jesus asking them to *change the concept of enemies within their hearts and minds* into *a concept of people who need mercy*? In other words, Jesus is asking them to change their concept of these people from *enemies* to *neighbors*, people who live *near to them*. When Jesus finishes telling the story of the good Samaritan to the lawyer, he asks him, "Which of these three, do you think, was a *neighbor* to the man who fell into the hands of the robbers?"[44] When the lawyer says, "The one who showed him *mercy*," he has joined together Jesus' teaching about *loving one's neighbor as oneself* at the beginning of their conversation with Jesus' teaching about *loving one's enemies* and being *merciful as God is merciful* in the Sermon on the Plain.[45] This lawyer evidently had been listening closely to Jesus for some time! In response to the lawyer, Jesus renews what he has said to him earlier about *doing* by saying, "Go and *do likewise*." Luke's presentation of the parable of the good Samaritan, therefore, summarizes and recapitulates Jesus' teaching in the Sermon on the Plain as well as the initial conversation with the lawyer about what he must *do* to inherit eternal life.[46] Rather than being "close to the kingdom of God," as the scribe is in Mark, this lawyer is close to the heart of Jesus' teaching about *loving one's neighbor, loving one's*

---

40. Luke 9:54.
41. 2 Kgs 1:9–16.
42. Luke 9:55.
43. Luke 6:27, 36.
44. Luke 10:36.
45. Luke 10:27, 35–36.
46. Luke 10:25.

enemies, and *being merciful as God is merciful."* Now all that is left for him is to *"Go* and *do* likewise."[47]

Before we leave Jesus' parable about the Samaritan, there is one more thing we must notice when the Samaritan takes the wounded man to the inn. After taking initial care of the wounded man in the inn, on the next day the Samaritan gives the innkeeper two denarii, and tells him, "Take care of him; and when I come back, I will repay you whatever more you spend."[48] In other words, the Samaritan not only put oil and wine on the wounds of the man and took him to the inn to be cared for, but he also promised to pay money to the innkeeper for his further care of him. In the Sermon on the Plain, Jesus taught that a person should give to everyone who begs, expecting nothing in return.[49] In this instance, the Samaritan gave everything a person needed, including money, *without even being asked.* How ironic it is that the Samaritan, an enemy, has not only *loved* the Lord with all his heart, soul, strength, and mind, but also has been *the neighbor* by *giving money* to enact *loving one's neighbor as oneself.*

CONCLUSION

During this phase of our journey we have seen the expansion of *love* in Matthew and Luke. In Matthew, Jesus' interpretation in the Sermon on the Mount of the commandment, "Love your neighbor as yourself" as "Love your enemies and pray for those who persecute you" establishes an environment for Jesus' discussion of being *"perfect* as your heavenly Father is *perfect."* Thus, when the rich man comes to Jesus in Matthew asking how he can have eternal life, Jesus rehearses commandments to him, then tells him that if he wishes to be *perfect,* he must sell his possessions, give money to the poor, and come, follow him.

In Luke the stage is set for Jesus' enactment of his ministry of *mercy* by his Sermon on the Plain, which begins with blessings on the poor and woes on the rich that lead immediately to a discussion of "Love your enemies." This prepares the hearer/reader for how *love* works in contexts where people are one's enemy. Jesus then tells a story of *an enemy who loves.* Who would expect a Samaritan to care for a wounded man in a ditch? He even takes him to an inn to be cared for, and then he is willing to pay for the expenses

---

47. Luke 10:37.
48. Luke 10:34–35.
49. Luke 6:30.

the wounded man will incur in future days as he is recovering in the inn. If people we may perceive as enemies are able to show mercy, and give money, to an unnamed wounded man in a ditch, surely we should be able to do this as well! Indeed, perhaps we might even learn how to change the concept of particular people we perceive to be our enemies into a concept of them as people who need our love and mercy.

During this phase of our journey we have seen how "the enemy" seems to be different in Matthew and Luke. We have seen how Matthew presents Jesus' teaching as *reshaped Torah*, while Luke presents Jesus *showing* people how to *love* God, neighbors, and enemies through *reshaped Torah, prophetic speech,* and *challenging parables*. Both Matthew and Luke are interested in people *living a life of love*. Their approach to it by writing a gospel of the life, death, and resurrection of Jesus shows many differences. According to Stephen Fowl, these differences are the special way "God invites believers to deepen their knowledge of and friendship with God through repeated and ongoing engagement with scripture."[50] Let us turn now to letters of Paul, to see what special emphases he has when he talks about *love* as *a way of life*.

QUESTIONS FOR DISCUSSION

1. Does *loving* mean something somewhat different in Matthew and Luke when they present Jesus teaching that we must *love our enemies*? Or are they teaching the same thing?

2. Why would the gospel of Luke expand the command to "Love your neighbor" to "Love your enemies"?

3. Why do you think the gospel of Luke presents Jesus as teaching "Be *merciful*, just as your Father is *merciful*" (Luke 6:36), rather than "Be *perfect* as your heavenly Father is *perfect*" (Matt 5:48)?

4. Explain how the Lukan version of the beatitudes presents a different challenge than the beatitudes in Matthew. Why do you think the gospel of Luke has a different emphasis in the beatitudes and then adds woes after them? What do you think was happening in emerging Christianity that created a context where a major topic in Jesus' teaching in Luke is about wealth?

---

50. Fowl, "Christian Theological Interpretation," 183.

5. Do you think the focus on wealth in Deuteronomy and the Prophets may indicate an environment of people living close to one another in cities and towns, rather than apart from one another with large expanses of land between them? If so, why? If not, why not?

6. Do you agree that true prophets are regularly rejected while false prophets are liked by many people? If you agree, what is the nature of a true prophet? If you do not agree, why?

7. How does the episode in which Jesus tells the story of the Good Samaritan "summarize and capitulate" major teaching of Jesus in the Sermon on the Plain?

8. Do you think a good way to understand the story of the Good Samaritan is to think of it as challenging a person to change their concept of a particular enemy into a neighbor? Or is there a better way to understand the story?

9. What is the relation between the Sermon on the Plain in Luke and the story of the Samaritan in Luke 10?

4

Christ Jesus as God's Love in Letters of Paul

Now faith, hope, and love abide, these three;
and the greatest of these is love.[1]

IN THIS CHAPTER WE revisit the hiddenness of love in the coming of the kingdom of God in Mark. Having journeyed through the coming of God's love into the world as fulfillment of the Torah and the Prophets in Matthew, and Jesus' prophetic blessing of the poor and marginalized and announcement of the burden of wealth in Luke, we ask ourselves, "How did the apostle Paul forcefully bring *agapē love* into the center of *Christ*-believing speech and action?"

In this chapter the word *Christ* will be italicized to call attention to Paul's use of the Greek word *christos* to refer to Jesus as the *anointed* Messiah (Greek: *christos*) of Israel. We have seen in previous chapters how Mark, Matthew, and Luke contribute to the prominence of *agapē love* in Christianity. But their contributions are only a beginning point for our journey. Mark only subtly introduces *God's love* in the baptism and transfiguration of Jesus. But he also presents Jesus interacting with other Jews about commandments in the Torah that emphasize the importance of *loving God* and *loving one's neighbor as oneself*. We also saw how both Matthew and Luke

---

1. 1 Cor 13:13.

expand Jewish teaching about *loving God* and *loving one's neighbor* into *loving one's enemies*. As we journeyed through these writings, we reminded ourselves we were seeing expansion and reshaping of teaching about love in Judaism at the time of Jesus. We also observed how Jesus embodied and enacted those teachings in his own life and death. But in all of this we did not see any explicit statements about God's love for the world. Also, we did not see any explicit statement that God is love. So, how did God's love become so central to Christian speech and belief?

My father quoted verses of the apostle Paul regularly to me and my two brothers as we grew up. The irony is that I do not ever remember him saying, "I love you." He did sign his many letters to us later in life with "Love, Dad." But in direct conversation my father was afraid that if he praised us we would become proud. And "*Pride* is the greatest sin," he would say. My mother told me that shortly after they were married she told my father she loved him and he said, "You know our duty is first to love God and then we can love each other." This hurt my mother, and this approach did not help my father and mother build a bond of love with each other in their later lives. In public my father was always very kind and respectful to others, and he never wanted people to know that he and my mother regularly quarreled and said mean things to one another. The irony, of course, was that other people knew very well. I was embarrassed later in life when the couple who was our favorite youth advisors in Church talked freely about the way my mother and father fought with each other. How could someone who quoted the apostle Paul regularly not be loving to his wife? And why could he not tell his children directly that he loved them? I have never written about this before, and I feel strange writing about it now. But perhaps now that I am in the final decades of my life I should feel free to write about it.

My father regularly quoted, "All things work together for good *to them that love God.*" He always quoted it in the King James Version and emphasized the last clause. And then he would preach to us about it. When he preached to us, he would go on to the last clause, "to them who are called according to his purpose."[2] He never went on to the next verse, "For whom he did foreknow, he also did destinate," because we were Evangelical and not Presbyterian. And he never went on with, "And whom he called, them he also justified," because even though his grandmother was German Lutheran, my father did not emphasize justification by faith over "all things work together for good."

---

2. Rom 8:28.

CHRIST JESUS AS GOD'S LOVE IN LETTERS OF PAUL

I never thought about the fact that my father's favorite verse in Paul's writings contained the verb *agapān*, to love God. I only came to realize this when I first taught about "Human and Divine Love in the Bible" on Zoom during COVID-19. Indeed, Paul was one of the major contributors to the centrality of *love* in Christian speech, belief, and action. To explain this I invite you on a journey that includes additional aspects of the Greek Old Testament, which was a translation of the Hebrew Bible into Greek after Alexander the Great conquered the land of Israel and Egypt prior to 300 BCE. By the third century BCE so many Jews spoke Greek in Egypt that Jewish scribes produced an official translation of the Hebrew Bible into Greek. As the Greek Old Testament emerged, additional books were part of "that which was written" in the environment of emerging Christianity. My father never talked about these additional books, but I learned in graduate school how important they are for understanding the emergence of Christianity.

WISDOM (*SOPHIA*) *LOVES* THOSE WHO *LOVE* HER IN JEWISH TRADITION

One of the most important developments during the two centuries prior to Christianity was expansion of biblical Wisdom tradition by Hellenistic (Greek) Jewish writers. In other words, a major part of the expansion of the Hebrew Bible (Tanakh) in the Greek Old Testament was the addition of Wisdom of Solomon, Sirach, and Psalms of Solomon to the Hebrew Solomonic traditions of Proverbs and Song of Songs. In addition, the prophetic book of Jeremiah was expanded with Baruch, named after the scribe of Jeremiah. This means that additional wisdom books in the Greek Old Testament (see the display) presented the commandments of the Torah and the call to obedience by the Prophets in the form of poetic wisdom. From the point of view of the Wisdom books, the commandments in Torah and the word of God in the Prophets were *wisdom* God gave to Israel to enable them to live righteously according to God's covenant with Israel.

Careful study of the letters of Paul in this newer environment of interpretation shows that Jewish Wisdom tradition enabled Paul to take new steps with the concept of *the love of God*. Among other things, the concept of *the love of God* brought the life, death, and resurrection of *Christ* Jesus into the hearts of believers. For us to experience how this worked, let us continue our journey by using the Greek Old Testament to help us understand love in the letters of Paul.

Greek Old Testament (Apocrypha Books and Additions [in NRSV Study Bibles] in Bold)		
Historical Books	Poetic and Wisdom Books	Prophets
Torah	Psalms	Hosea
Genesis	**Psalm 151**	Amos
Exodus	Proverbs	Micah
Leviticus	Ecclesiastes	Joel
Numbers	Song of Songs	Obadiah
Deuteronomy	Job	Jonah
Joshua	**Wisdom of Solomon**	Nahum
Judges	**Sirach (Ben Sira,**	Habakkuk
Ruth	**Ecclesiasticus)**	Zephaniah
1–2 Kings (1–2 Samuel)	**Psalms of Solomon**	Haggai
3–4 Kings (1–2 Kings)		Zechariah
1–2 Chronicles		Malachi
Prayer of Manasseh		Isaiah
1 Esdras (Ezra, Nehemiah)		Jeremiah
2 Esdras		**Baruch**
Esther (**additions**)		**Bar 6 = Epistle of Jeremiah**
Judith		Lamentations
Tobith		Ezekiel
1–2 Maccabees		Daniel (**additions below**)
3 Maccabees (not in Roman Catholic Canon)		**Prayer of Azariah**
4 Maccabees (only in appendix to Greek Bible)		**Song of the Three Jews**
		Susanna
1 Enoch (Ethiopian Canon only; also among Qumran Dead Sea Scrolls)		**Bel and the Dragon**

In the book of 1 Kings in the Greek Old Testament (see the display), Solomon son of David, king of Israel, prays for wisdom to come into him and guide him. In the Greek version the verb *agapān* occurs as it describes Solomon's relation to the Lord:

> Solomon loved (*ēgapēse*) the Lord, walking in the ordinances of his father David . . . And God said, "Ask some petition for yourself." And Solomon said, ". . . Give your servant a heart to hear and to judge your people with righteousness to discern between good and evil . . ." And the Lord said to him, "Because you have requested this thing from me . . . behold, I have given you a prudent and wise (*sophēn*) heart; like there has not been in anyone like you before you, and after you there shall not arise another like you."[3]

3. 1 Kgs 3:3, 5, 9–12 LXX auth. trans.

Christ Jesus as God's Love in Letters of Paul

This prayer for wisdom in 1 Kings was expanded in Wisdom of Solomon, a book in the Old Testament Apocrypha, to describe Solomon's *love* of Wisdom (see the display),

> I loved (*ephilēsa*) her [Wisdom] and sought her from my youth;
> I desired to take her for my bride,
> and became enamored of her beauty.
> She glorifies her noble birth by living with God,
> and the Lord of all loves (*ēgapēsen*) her.[4]

Here we see not only that Solomon *loved* Wisdom but also that the Lord *loves* Wisdom. Indeed, Wisdom *lives* with God and sits by God's throne! This presence of *love* in the relation of God to Wisdom is very important for Paul's thinking about the relation of *Christ* Jesus to God. But let us continue with Solomon as he explains his earlier years in relation to his days as an adult king:

> As a child I was naturally gifted,
> and a good soul fell to my lot,
> or rather, being good, I entered an undefiled body.
> But I perceived that I would not possess wisdom unless God gave her to me—
> and it was a mark of insight to know whose gift she was—
> so I appealed to the Lord and implored him,
> and with my whole heart I said,
> "O God of my ancestors and Lord of mercy,
> who have made all things by your word (*logōi*),
> and by your wisdom (*sophiāi*) have formed humankind
> to have dominion over the creatures you have made,
> and rule the world in holiness and righteousness
> and pronounce judgment in uprightness of soul,
> give me the wisdom (*sophian*) that sits by your throne,
> and do not reject me from among your children."[5]

Perhaps the most remarkable thing is that the book of Proverbs in the Old Testament personifies *sophia* so fully that she becomes a speaking-acting presence on earth. In Proverbs, "Wisdom sings aloud in passageways, and in the village squares speaks boldly. And she makes proclamation on the top of the walls, and sits by the gates of princes; and at the gates of the

---

4. Wis 8:2.
5. Wis 8:19—9:4.

city boldly speaks out."⁶ From her dwelling places on earth Wisdom cries out as a woman who raises her voice and says, "To you, O people, I call, and my cry is to all who live." As she continues she says, "I love (*agapō*) those who love (*philountas*) me, and those who seek me diligently will find me."⁷ In Proverbs and Wisdom of Solomon, then, Wisdom is personified as a woman who speaks directly to hearers. In the Greek Old Testament, Wisdom is *sophia*. As she speaks about righteousness and understanding, she says that she herself *loves* those who love her. In addition, God *loves* her and daily she brings joy to God as she lives with God.

There is yet one more step we must take in our journey with Greek Old Testament Wisdom before turning to Paul's letters. In Sirach, Wisdom not only invites people to come to her but she tells her story of how she got from heaven to earth:

> I came forth from the mouth of the Most High
>   and covered the earth like a mist.
> I encamped in the heights,
>   and my throne was in a pillar of cloud.
> Alone I compassed the vault of heaven
>   and traversed the depths of the abyss.
> Over waves of the sea, over all the earth,
>   and over every people and nation I have held sway.
> Among all these I sought a resting place;
>   in whose territory should I abide?
> Then the Creator of all things gave me a command,
>   and my Creator pitched my tent (*skēnēn*).
> He said, "Encamp (*kataskēnōson*) in Jacob,
>   and in Israel receive your inheritance."⁸

In Sirach, Wisdom tells how she was created before the beginning of heaven and earth. She was the mist that hovered over the waters in Gen 1:2, and after God created the heavens and the earth she journeyed throughout all the cosmos. Then she was in a pillar of cloud that appeared at various times throughout the history of Israel. Then she came and *tented* on earth. At this point she obeyed God's command to *tent* among Jacob/Israel. At this point, we get a glimpse of how Paul and the gospel of John could move toward a view that God's wisdom came to the earth as *Christ*-Messiah Jesus and

6. Prov 1:20–21 LXX auth. trans.
7. Prov 8:4, 8, 14, 17 LXX auth. trans.
8. Sir 24:3–8.

tented on earth. From Wisdom's location within Israel she calls people to her:

> Come to me, you who desire me,
>   and eat your fill of my fruits.
> For the memory of me is sweeter than honey,
>   and the possession of me sweeter than the honeycomb.
> Those who eat of me will hunger for more,
>   and those who drink of me will thirst for more.
> Whoever obeys me will not be put to shame,
>   and those who work (*ergazomenoi*) with me will not sin.[9]

Here it is important to see that Wisdom does various kinds of *work* (*erga*) on earth as well as throughout the cosmos. On earth, she "*calls* people to action," "works *with* people" and asks people to "work *with* her." We will see in future chapters that Wisdom becomes more and more a cosmic energy-force throughout the cosmos. This will become especially important as we discuss aspects of the gospel of John. But for now, let us turn to Paul's letter of 1 Corinthians to see how *wisdom* and *love* intertwine in Paul's statements.

CHRIST JESUS IS GOD'S WISDOM FOR THOSE WHO *LOVE* GOD

In the opening chapter of 1 Corinthians Paul distinguishes between God's wisdom and human wisdom. As he develops his argument, instead of arguing that "something greater than Solomon is here," as Jesus himself states in Matt 12:42 and Luke 11:31, Paul says, "*Christ* Jesus . . . became for us *wisdom* (*sophia*) from God."[10] For Paul, God's wisdom came to earth, took the human form of *Christ* Jesus, and *tented* in earthly time and space. Then Paul describes how *Christ* Jesus is God's wisdom for *those who love God,* and how he as an apostle of *Christ* Jesus speaks God's Wisdom *among the mature*:

> Yet among the mature (*teleiois*) we do speak wisdom (*sophian*), though it is not a wisdom (*sophian*) of this age or of the rulers of this age, who are being destroyed. But we speak God's wisdom (*sophian*), a hidden mystery (*mystēriōi*), which God decreed before the ages for our glory and which none of the rulers of this

---

9. Sir 24:19–22.

10. 1 Cor 1:30. *Christ* is italicized throughout this chapter, since *Christ* is Paul's special name for Jesus either by itself or as *Christ* Jesus or Jesus *Christ*.

age understood, for if they had, they would not have crucified the Lord of glory. But, as it is written,

> "What no eye has seen, nor ear heard,
> nor the human heart conceived,
> what God has prepared for those who love (*agapōsin*) him"—
> God has revealed (*apekalypsen*) to us through the Spirit,
> for the Spirit searches everything,
> even the depths of God.[11]

Here Paul explains that those who *love* God have *Christ* Jesus *revealed* to them as God's wisdom who came and was crucified as *the Lord of glory*. In other words, the crucifixion reveals God's power, wisdom, and glory *to those who love God*, rather than being a story of weakness, foolishness, and shame. So far so good. My father would love all of this about Paul. He loved that Paul taught mature wisdom. In fact, he thought even little boys should give up their childish ways and become little men. He was, in fact, quite successful in this way with me and my two brothers. It was our duty already by age six to milk at least one cow by hand in the evening after we came home from school. By age ten we started driving a tractor, by age fourteen we had school permits to drive back and forth to high school, which was nine miles away on gravel roads. So here we see Paul's mature wisdom, which is really a revision of the Shema of Israel that focuses on *loving* God with all of one's heart, soul, mind, and strength. But how does Paul move into a discussion of *loving one another*?

FILLING LOVE (*AGAPĒ*) WITH UPBUILDING VIRTUES

The next step Paul makes is to personify *love*. In his letters, Paul never makes *love* into a *personage who speaks,* as Wisdom becomes in biblical tradition. But Paul personifies *love* by giving *love* human attributes and characteristics. The earliest moment in Paul's letter when Paul does this is 1 Corinthians 8, when Paul distinguishes between knowledge (*gnōsis*) and *love* (*agapē*). For Paul, everyone possesses knowledge. Then he says, "Knowledge *puffs up*, but love *builds up* (*oikodomei*)."[12] When Paul speaks in this way he personifies both knowledge and love by making them subjects of action. Personifying knowledge is not a huge step for Paul, of course, since

---

11. 1 Cor 2:6–10; quoting a blending of LXX Isa 64:3(4) and Sir 1:10.
12. 1 Cor 8:1.

knowledge is intimately related to wisdom. But for Paul *true knowledge* must have the humility of knowing there are things, especially about God, we cannot know. He calls this "God's wisdom, a hidden mystery."[13] This emphasis on the humility of not knowing leads Paul to contrast *knowledge* with *love* rather than *wisdom*. For Paul, *love* is humble rather than puffed up. To get to this thinking, Paul first describes himself and his followers as *fools*, people who are opposite from *wise*. Some of the *Christ*-believers in Corinth were causing problems with their claim to have greater *wisdom* than others. In relation to them, Paul says:

> *We* [Paul and Apollos] *are fools for the sake of Christ*, but you are sensible people in *Christ*. We are weak, but you are strong. You are honored, but we are dishonored. To the present hour we are hungry and thirsty, we are naked and beaten and homeless, and we grow weary from the work of our own hands. When reviled, we bless; when persecuted, we endure; when slandered, we speak kindly. We have become like the rubbish of the world, the dregs of all things, to this very day.[14]

As Paul searches for an alternative to *fools*, he chooses *love*. *Love* is humble. But instead of starting with humility, Paul builds on assertions he makes in the early chapters in 1 Corinthians.

The highpoint of Paul's presentation of *love*, as many will know, comes in 1 Corinthians 13. First Paul distinguishes between *having* or *not having love* in a way that is related to Solomon's distinction between *having or not having wisdom*:

> If I speak in the tongues of humans and of angels but *do not have love* (*agapēn*), I am a noisy gong or a clanging cymbal. And if I have prophetic powers and understand all mysteries and all knowledge and if I have all faith so as to remove mountains but *do not have love* (*agapēn*), I am *nothing* (*ouden*). If I give away all my possessions and if I hand over my body so that I may boast but *do not have love* (*agapēn*), I gain *nothing* (*ouden*).[15]

When Solomon tells his story in Wisdom of Solomon, he says he knew that he would not have wisdom unless God gave her to him.[16] So he prayed to God to give him wisdom:

13. 1 Cor 2:7.
14. 1 Cor 4:10–13.
15. 1 Cor 13:1–3.
16. Wis 8:21.

> Give me the wisdom (*sophian*) that sits by your throne,
>   and do not reject me from among your children.
> For I am your servant, the son of your female servant,
>   a man who is weak and short-lived,
>   with little understanding of judgment and laws,
> for even one who is perfect (*teleios*) among humans
>   will be *regarded as nothing* (*ouden*) without the wisdom
>   (*sophias*) that comes from you.[17]

Solomon wanted to *have wisdom* so he could judge between right and wrong. Without God's wisdom he would be *regarded as nothing*. Without *love*, Paul says, he is nothing, just as Solomon was nothing without wisdom. Moreover, Paul wants every member of the community to *have love* so there is "no dissension within the body." Without love, the members of the community will not care for one another. Paul desires that all the members may have *love* so they "have the same care for one another. If one member suffers, all suffer together with it; if one member is honored, all rejoice together with it."[18] For Paul, when we care for one another through *love*, all things are done "for building up."[19]

When Paul continues in chapter 13, he *personifies love*. And here is a challenge for translators. *Agapē* is a feminine noun in Greek, just as *sophia* is a feminine noun. Greek verbs contain *within themselves* first, second, or third person, so it is not necessary for a Greek writer to supply a pronoun.[20] A straightforward translation of 1 Cor 13: 4–7 into English without supplying pronouns that are not in the Greek wording of Paul's letter looks like this:

> Love (*agapē*) is patient; love (*agapē*) is kind, is not jealous;
> love (*agapē* is not boastful, is not puffed up (*physioutai*),
> does not behave in an unseemly manner, is not self-seeking,
> is not irritable, keeps no record of wrong,
> does not rejoice in wrongdoing but rejoices in the truth, bears all things,
> believes all things, hopes all things, endures all things.[21]

---

17. Wis 9:4–6.
18. 1 Cor 12:25–26.
19. 1 Cor 14:3–5, 12, 17.
20. Sometimes a Greek writer supplies the pronoun *I, you (sg.), he, she, it, we, you (pl.),* or *they* along with the verb for emphasis and at other times the writer does not.
21. Author's translation. First Corinthians 13:4–7 contains the feminine noun with article *hē agapē* as the repeated subject of the first two verbs and perhaps the fourth verb in 13:4. Throughout 13:5–7 there is no pronoun subject for emphasis.

Since this is such a long string of verbs, translators regularly add a pronoun at one or more places. The NRSVue translation supplies *it* at five places:

1) *It* does not insist on 2) *its* own way;
3) *It* keeps no record of wrongs;
4) *It* does not rejoice in wrongdoing but rejoices in the truth.
5) *It* bears all things, believes all things, endures all things.²²

If a translator adopts the feminine gender pronoun for the subject *agapē*, like the feminine pronoun regularly is adopted for *sophia* wisdom, the pronoun will be *she*. This produces a translation like this:

> Love is patient; love is kind,
>   is not jealous;
> love is not boastful,
>   is not puffed up,
> She does not behave in an unseemly manner,
>   is not self-seeking,
> She is not irritable,
>   keeps no record of wrongs,
> She does not rejoice in wrongdoing
>   but rejoices in the truth.
> She bears all things, believes all things,
>   hopes all things, endures all things.²³

Why do translators use *it* rather than *she*? Some would argue that love is simply an abstract noun, and thus should be translated *it*. But is *love* simply an abstract noun in the thinking of Paul? What if *love* is closely related to *wisdom* in Paul's thinking? In Romans Paul says, "Love (*agapē*) works (*ergazetai*) no wrong to a neighbor."²⁴ Doesn't this seem like *love* is an acting spirit-force with a significant relation to *wisdom* in the Jewish thinking of Paul's time?

An important thing about the description of *love* in 1 Corinthians 13 is its relation to Paul's discussion in previous chapters. Paul starts with *love* as *patient* and *kind*, two words he does not use anywhere else in the letter. But then he introduces a series of *negatives*. When Paul uses negatives, he is making the content of *love* into *Christ*-wisdom that builds up

---

22. 1 Cor 13:4–7.
23. 1 Cor 13:4–7 auth. trans.
24. Rom 13:10 auth. trans.

the community. Instead of putting the guidelines into the form of commandments ("Do . . . ; do not . . .), Paul puts them in the form of "*Love* does . . . and *love* does not . . ." In this way Paul fills *love* with actions he desires among *Christ*-believers. With this move Paul has transformed the Torah and the Prophets into *Christ*-oriented *love* action.

Paul's list of negatives begins with *jealousy*: "Love is *not jealous* (*zēloi*)." Earlier, Paul has discussed jealousy as a problem among the Corinthians, and he considers it to be a source of disagreements among them. In 1 Cor 3:2–3 he says:

> I fed you with milk, not solid food, for you were not ready for solid food. Even now you are still not ready, for you are still fleshly. For as long as there is jealousy (*zēlos*) and quarreling among you, are you not fleshly, and behaving according to human inclinations?"

Love, Paul says in 1 Cor 13:4, does not act with jealousy, nor does she quarrel. If the Corinthians had love they would be *spiritual*. Instead, they are *fleshly*. They are infants in *Christ* rather than mature adults (*teleios*) in *Christ*.

Second, Paul says, "*Love* is not boastful, *is not puffed up*." Paul has much to say about boasting, *being puffed up*, in previous chapters. Paul begins by asserting:

> If you think that you are wise in this age, you should become
> fools so that you may become wise. For the wisdom of this world
> is foolishness with God. For it is written,
>
> > "He catches the wise in their craftiness,"
> > and again,
> > "The Lord knows the thoughts of the wise,
> > that they are futile."
>
> So let no one boast about people. For all things are yours, whether Paul or Apollos or Cephas or the world or life or death or the present or the future—all are yours, and you are *Christ's*, and *Christ* is God's.[25]

---

25. 1 Cor 3:18–23.

Love	
Patient	
Kind	
Jealous	Not jealous
Boastful	Not Boastful
Puffed up	Not puffed up
Behaves in an unseemly manner	Does not behave in an unseemly manner
Seeks her own advantage	Does not seek her own advantage
Irritable	Not irritable
Keeps record of wrongdoing (*kakon*)	Does not keep record of wrongdoing (*kakon*)
Rejoices in wrongdoing (*adikia*)	Rejoices in the truth (*alētheia*)
Bears (*stegein*) all things	
Believes (*pisteuein*) all things	
Endures (*hypomonein*) all things	

After quoting *what is written* to explain to the Corinthians that "the wisdom of this world is foolishness with God," Paul tells them that he, Apollos, and Peter are *servants of Christ* and *stewards of God's mysteries*, and then he says:

> I have applied all this to Apollos and myself for your benefit, brothers and sisters, so that you may learn through us what "Not beyond what is written" means, so that none of you *will be puffed up* in favor of one against another.[26]

Then later Paul says:

> But some of you, thinking that I am not coming to you, have become *puffed up*. But I will come to you soon, if the Lord wills, and I will find out not the talk of these *puffed up* people but their power.[27]

When Paul addresses the immorality of a man living with his father's wife, he says:

---

26. 1 Cor 3:4:6.
27. 1 Cor 4:18–20 auth. trans.

Finding Love

> And you are *puffed up*! Should you not rather have mourned, so that he who has done this would have been removed from among you?[28]

Then four chapters later he says:

> Now concerning food sacrificed to idols: we know that "all of us possess knowledge." Knowledge *puffs up*, but *love builds up*. Anyone who claims to know something does not yet have the necessary knowledge; but anyone who *loves* (*agapāi*) God is known by him.[29]

This is the first moment in Paul's letter when he personalizes *love* as a subject that *builds up* rather than *puffs up* or causes *quarreling* or *disagreements* in the community. And it is also the moment when Paul talks about God *knowing* a person when that person *loves* God. Paul returns to this thought in chapter thirteen after he has described *love*, when he says:

> When I was a child, I spoke like a child, I thought like a child, I reasoned like a child. When I became an adult, I put an end to childish ways. For now we see only a reflection, as in a mirror, but then we will see face to face. Now I know only in part; then I will know fully, even as I have been fully known. And now faith, hope, and *love* remain, these three, and the greatest of these is *love*.[30]

At this point, let us recall that Solomon said:

> As a child I was naturally gifted,
> and a good soul fell to my lot;
> or rather, being good, I entered an undefiled body.
> But I perceived that I would not possess wisdom unless God gave her to me.[31]

This is a statement by the *adult* Solomon talking about himself as a *child*. When Paul talks about his childhood, he talks about receiving *mature* (*teleios*) *wisdom* that possesses *love* within it. When Paul received *love* in his wisdom, he became *fully known* by God. For humans to claim they have all knowledge, therefore, is a problem. Knowledge is limited by the hidden, mysterious nature of God's wisdom. What people need is *love*, and when

---

28. 1 Cor 5:2 auth. trans.
29. 1 Cor 8:1–3.
30. 1 Cor 13:11–13.
31. Wis 8:19.

they have *love* within their wisdom they become fully known by God. So Paul's ministry is a ministry of *love*. When he describes this ministry, he includes many of the dispositions and actions he includes when he describes *love* in 1 Corinthians 13. So how can a person *receive* love? Solomon prayed for wisdom, and God gave it to him. How does Paul think *love* comes into believers. Let us turn to Romans and Galatians to see what Paul says.

CHRIST IS GOD'S LOVE POURED INTO BELIEVING HEARTS BY THE HOLY SPIRIT

A major question is how *love* gets into our bodies. Again, knowing Jewish Wisdom tradition helps us. Wisdom is a spirit that is holy and only-begotten. Wisdom loves the good, loves humanity, and is beneficially active both throughout the cosmos and within human beings. This is how Wisdom is presented in Wisdom of Solomon:

> There is in her [*sophia*] a knowing spirit (*pneuma noeron*)
> that is holy, only begotten (*monogenes*), manifold,
>   subtle, beneficially mobile (*eukineton*), clear,
> unpolluted, distinct, invulnerable,
>   loving the good (*philagathon*),
> keen, irresistible,
>   beneficially active (*euergetikon*),
> loving humanity (*philanthrōpon*), steadfast,
>   sure, free from anxiety, all-powerful,
> overseeing all, and penetrating through all spirits (*pneumatōn*)
>   that are knowing (*noeron*), pure,
> and altogether subtle.[32]

In addition:

> Although she [*sophia*] is but one,
>   she can do all things,
> and while remaining (*menousa*) in herself,
>   she renews all things;
> in every generation she passes into holy souls
>   and makes them friends (*philous*) of God and prophets;
> for God loves (*agapāi*) nothing so much as the person who lives
>   with (*synoikounta*) wisdom.[33]

---

32. Wis 7:22–23 auth. trans.
33. Wis 7:27–28.

Finding Love

As Paul expands on the relation of God to *Christ* in Romans, he introduces special activity by the Holy Spirit:

> Hope does not put us to shame, because God's *love* has been poured into our hearts through the Holy Spirit that has been given to us. For while we were still weak, at the right time *Christ* died for the ungodly. Indeed, rarely will anyone die for a righteous person—though perhaps for a good person someone might actually dare to die. But God proves God's *love* for us in that while we still were sinners *Christ* died for us.[34]

Here Paul has reconfigured *Christ as God's wisdom* into *Christ as God's love* that "has been poured into our hearts through the Holy Spirit that has been given to us." Paul has filled *God's love* with the story of *Christ's* crucifixion, death, and resurrection. Then Paul says the Holy Spirit has poured this story of love into the hearts of those who believe.

For Paul, the heart guides both the mind and the actions. So as Paul talks about *Christ* as God's love within the body of a believer in Philippians, he uses words closely aligned with his description of *love* in 1 Corinthians 13:

> If, then, there is any comfort in *Christ*, any consolation from *love* (*agapēs*), any partnership in the Spirit, any tender affection and sympathy, make my joy complete: be of the same mind, having the same *love* (*agapēn*), being in full accord and of one mind. Do nothing from selfish ambition or empty conceit, but in humility regard others as better than yourselves. Let each of you look not to your own interests, but to the interests of others. Let the same mind be in you that was in *Christ* Jesus.[35]

When Paul talks about the presence of the story of *Christ* in his own life in Galatians, he becomes even more personal:

> I have been crucified with *Christ*, and it is no longer I who live, but it is *Christ* who lives in me. And the life I now live in the flesh I live by the faith of the Son of God, who *loved* (*agapēsantos*) me and gave himself for me.[36]

For Paul, the story of *Christ* lives within him much like the story of God's wisdom lived within Solomon. But Paul emphasizes that *Christ* is *God's love*

---

34. Rom 5:5, 8.
35. Phil 2:1–5.
36. Gal 2:19–20.

and this *love* is especially present in *Christ's* death and resurrection which the Holy Spirit has poured into his heart.

As Paul develops his understanding of *God's love* through *Christ*, he coins the phrase "*the love of Christ.*" When Paul does this, he has shortened the phrase "the *love* of God in *Christ* Jesus our Lord" to "*the love of Christ.*" Here we see the intimate relation of the *love of God* to *Jesus as God's love* that came to the earth in the form of *Christ* Jesus who died, was raised, and now is at the right hand of God.[37] Then this is the moment when Paul brings the attributes of the death and exaltation of Christ into *the love of Christ*:

> Who will separate us from *the love of Christ*?
> Will affliction or distress or persecution or famine or nakedness or peril or sword? As it is written,
>
> "For your sake we are being killed all day long;
> we are accounted as sheep to be slaughtered."
>
> No, in all these things we are more than victorious through him who *loved* us.
> For I am convinced that neither death, nor life, nor angels, nor rulers, nor things present, nor things to come, nor powers, nor height, nor depth, nor anything else in all creation will be able to separate us from the *love of God in Christ Jesus our Lord*.[38]

This cherished passage in the New Testament exhibits Paul's reconfiguration of *Christ* Jesus as *God's wisdom* into *Christ* Jesus as *God's love*. Christ not only journeyed through the cosmos to come and *tent* on earth as God's wisdom does, but Christ came to earth, died, was raised, and sits at the right hand of God as *God's love*. Who, then, can separate believers from *the love of Christ*? Can death or life, or anything in the cosmos *separate* believers from *Christ's love*? No. Just as God's Wisdom became present on earth, so in Paul's *messianic* (*christos*-oriented) thinking *God's love in Christ Jesus* became present on earth to give special benefits to those who believe.

CONCLUSION

This step in our journey has prepared us for the next chapter, where *God's love* exists explicitly in the flesh of the Son who laid down his life and took it up again in the gospel of John. In this chapter we have taken a journey with

---

37. Rom 8:34.
38. Rom 8:35–39.

Wisdom, who entered into Solomon so he could judge between right and wrong. And we also have seen how Wisdom became a personage who journeyed throughout the cosmos before she came to *tent* among the people of Israel. Within Israel she called people to her, and those who found her also found life.

After taking this journey with Wisdom in the Greek Old Testament, we turned to Paul's letters. Paul begins with *Christ* as "God's wisdom, a hidden mystery, which God decreed before the ages for our glory."[39] But then Paul transforms God's wisdom into *love* that *builds up*. When Paul describes the inner nature of *love* in 1 Corinthians 13, *love* functions as the personified spirit-agent within humans who does the proper things that *build up the community* and does not do the things that cause quarreling and disagreements in the community. In Paul's thought, then, active *love* replaces the commandments of the Torah and the calls to obedience in the Prophets by being God's spirit-power that enables believers to *build up* the community. Then Paul takes one more step. He fills *love* with the story of *Christ's* death, resurrection, and exaltation to the right hand of God. This *story of God's love*, Paul says in Romans, is *poured* into the hearts of believers by the Holy Spirit. Then Paul says in Galatians that *Christ lives in him*. This is so real to him that he can say, "I have been crucified with *Christ*," and he can also say, "*Christ loved* me."[40]

In this chapter, then, we have seen how Paul filled *agapē love* with the actions for building up and caring for *Christ*-believers in the communities to whom he ministered. Also, we have seen how *God's love* in the story of *Christ's* death, resurrection, and exaltation comes into the hearts of believers through the Holy Spirit. In the next chapter, we will see how the story of *God's love* becomes the story of Logos Jesus, the Son, *tenting* on earth. This story will bring *God's love* even more into the center of belief both for the New Testament and for the lives of Christians in future centuries up to our present day.

---

39. 1 Cor 2:7.
40. Gal 2:19–20.

QUESTIONS FOR DISCUSSION

1. What is your reaction to the personification of Wisdom in biblical tradition? Why do you think Wisdom came to be personified in the tradition of Israel?

2. Why do you think it would have been natural for many of the additional books in the Greek Old Testament to be Wisdom books? What do you understand to be happening in the Mediterranean world that may have contributed to this additional development of wisdom in the Septuagint?

3. Are you surprised by the way in which Paul understands *Christ* as God's wisdom? In other words, are there other ways in which Paul could have emphasized *Christ* as God's wisdom?

4. Do you think it is a good thing to supply *she* rather than *it* for *love* in 1 Corinthians 13:4–7, or does it not make much difference for you?

5. Do the functions of *love* in 1 Corinthians give you any new ideas about *Christ* as the fulfilment of the Torah and the Prophets? Does *love* as Paul develops it make it natural for Christians to consider *love* to be a transformation of the Torah and Prophets?

6. Do you see Paul creating a *love* ethic for communities? If you see him doing this, can you explain how he does it? If you do not see Paul focusing on love in community life, explain why you do not.

7. Did this chapter give you any new ideas about how "the story of Jesus" can be brought into the lives of believers? Can you describe similarities between the function of love in the synoptic gospels and Paul's letters of 1–2 Corinthians, Romans, and Galatians? How would you describe differences between them?

5

Love, Life, and Friendship in the Gospel of John

> Jesus said, "No one has greater love than this, to lay down one's life for one's friends."[1]

IN THE PRECEDING CHAPTER we saw the apostle Paul asserting that *Christ* Jesus was killed, buried, and raised by God to bring everlasting life to *Christ*-believers. In other words, Paul says that everlasting life comes to believers as a result of *things that happened to Jesus*. Paul does not say that everlasting life comes to believers because of things *Christ* Jesus *said*. In his view, people who *believe* that Jesus, who did not look like a powerful Messiah, *is* God's Messiah (*christos*) receive everlasting life through God's raising of *Christ* (his Messiah) from the dead.

In the gospel of John, in contrast to Paul, everything Jesus *says* is of extreme importance. Indeed, *the all-important* thing in John is to *believe* what Jesus *says*. Then *doing* follows from what Jesus *says*. In John, those who *believe* what Jesus *says, understand* what he says as *commandments*. Those *who obey those commandments* receive everlasting life. In other words, Jesus' *words* give everlasting life, *if* a person *does* them. This sounds like the gospel of John takes us back to the Jewish world of the synoptic gospels, right? This is where the surprise comes.

---

1. John 15:13.

Love, Life, and Friendship in the Gospel of John

The gospel of John is very different from Mark, Matthew, and Luke. Most people know this, but how different is it? There is no Sermon on the Mount or Sermon on the Plain in John. No rich man comes to Jesus to ask him what he must do to inherit everlasting life. Jesus has no conversation where he or anyone recites the Jewish Shema. Jesus never teaches that people must love their enemies. In the gospel of John, John the Baptist tells people about Jesus' baptism, but he does not say a divine voice came out of heaven saying that Jesus is God's beloved son. There is no transfiguration of Jesus on a mountain in John. In chapter three, however, there is a verse that virtually all Christians my age know by heart in the King James version: "For God so loved the world that he gave his only-begotten Son that whosoever believeth in him should not perish, but have everlasting life." And most know this is John 3:16.

So, what is the big change? The answer is that the gospel of John asks hearers to *believe a cosmic story about the Father and the Son*. This chapter is devoted to setting forth features of this cosmic story related to *agapē love*. John 3:16 tells the hearer some of the major features of the story. One of the most important things about John 3:16 is the phrase "only-begotten Son." In John, the Father gives *the only-begotten Son* many tasks he must *do* before *all* is finished.[2] And these are *cosmic* tasks, namely tasks performed in the entire universe. How did the tasks of Jesus become so different from the synoptic gospels? The answer lies in some minor changes and some major changes in early Christian thinking, belief, and storytelling.

Mark, Matthew, and Luke have the divine voice at Jesus' baptism revealing to Jesus that he is God's *beloved* Son. So a basic framework is set here for Christian storytelling about God's *love* for Jesus. The letters of Paul also refer to Jesus as God's Son, but Paul does not emphasize that God *loves* his *Son*. Rather, Paul emphasizes that God *raised* his *Messiah, Christ* Jesus, from the dead and in this context the Spirit *pours* God's love into the hearts of believers. The gospel of John, in contrast, never refers to Jesus with Paul's favorite name *Christ* Jesus, even though this gospel knows that Jesus is the Messiah and twice refers to Jesus as Jesus *Christ*.[3] The most important name for Jesus in the gospel of John is *the Son*, which is an abbreviation of *the only-begotten Son of God*.[4] And in John focus on *the Son* is a *huge* part of the change.

2. John 17:4; 19:30.
3. John 1:17; 17:3.
4. John 3:18: *ho monogenos huios tou theou*.

Finding Love

John 3:16 says that God so loved the world that he *gave* his only Son. *Gave* him to what? This statement is an initial introduction to *the cosmic story* that becomes the special focus of *belief* in the gospel of John. The story starts with God and tells the reader that God *loves* the *cosmos*, a Greek word regularly translated as *the world*. We must notice that this is quite opposite to where the Jewish Shema starts: "You shall *love* the Lord your God." For the gospel of John, the story does not start with the *love* of humans for God, but with the *love* of God for the *cosmos*, where humans *live*. The *cosmic story* in John 3:16 continues with God *so loving the cosmos* that he "*gave* his only Son." This is very interesting language, which we did not see in the synoptic gospels or in the letters of Paul discussed in the previous chapter. We must explore this *giving* by God a bit more before we proceed further.

One of the most interesting assertions about *giving* in the gospel of Mark, which we discussed in the first chapter, is Jesus' statement to the disciples that to them "*has been given* the mystery of the kingdom of God."[5] Since this *giving* is in passive voice, this probably means that *God gave* Jesus' disciples the mystery of the kingdom of God. When Paul talks about *God's wisdom, secret and hidden* in 1 Cor 2:7, he does not talk about *giving*. Rather, Paul says that God's wisdom has been *revealed (apekalypsen)* to us through the Spirit.[6] For Paul, God uses the Spirit as an agent both to *reveal God's wisdom* to humans on earth and to *pour* love into our hearts. In the gospel of John, instead of God using the Spirit to *pour* love and to *reveal God's wisdom*, God *gives* his Son to humans by *sending his word (logos)* as the *only-begotten* who *tents* on earth both *with* and *in* humans.[7] In John, God's Son is God's Word, and the emphasis is that *the Word has life* in it and has the power to *give everlasting life* to all who *believe* in the Son. In other words, while Paul talks about *having love*, the gospel of John talks about *having everlasting life*. So how does *having everlasting life* become such a central focus in John? The answer lies in the reconfiguration of the Genesis creation story in the prologue to John. So let us go to the opening verses of the gospel of John.

---

5. Mark 4:11.

6. 1 Cor 2:7–10.

7. For the *tenting* of Logos Jesus on earth, see *eskēnōsen* in John 1:14. The word *revealed* occurs only once in John when the narrator quotes the LXX version of Isa 53:1: "Lord, who has believed our message, and to whom has the arm of the Lord been revealed (*apekalyphthē*)." This is not Johannine language but language from the Greek Old Testament.

Love, Life, and Friendship in the Gospel of John

LIFE-FLOW IN THE PROLOGUE TO JOHN

The opening words of the gospel of John introduce the *cosmic story* that presents the Johannine story about the Father and the Son to readers. The story in the gospel of John reconfigures the Jewish story of Wisdom, but it reconfigures it in a different way than Paul does. Instead of Jesus being God's *wisdom* who became *Christos* Jesus, God's *wisdom* becomes God's *word* (*logos*) in the gospel of John. As the *cosmic story* unfolds, this means that believers must *keep* the words of the Son as *commandments*. For now we need to see how *the words* of *the Son give everlasting life*.

The focus on Jesus as God's *word* that brings *life* comes out of a Johannine *interpretation* of the story of God's creation of the world in the first chapter of Genesis. Where Genesis says, "God *said*, 'Let there be light,'" the gospel of John says "the light *shines* (*phainei*) in the darkness." For John this means that light *manifested itself* in the darkness. The question is how and where light *manifests itself*. In John, *the word* (*logos*) is the *true light* (*alēthinon phōs*), and this light *came* to *enlighten* (*phōtizei*) the world.[8] This means that *word* manifests itself as *everlasting light* that *enlightens through word in the created world*. Thus, when *the word* becomes flesh in the world, *the words* of the Son Jesus Christ *enlighten* human beings who *believe* the words.

Then the prologue to John takes another step that is central to belief in the Johannine *cosmic story*. *In the word* was *life* (*zōē*). We must spend a little time with Genesis to see how *life* is *in the word* and becomes so central to the Johannine *cosmic story*. In the first chapter of Genesis, after God said, "Light," God said, "waters" and "earth," and these *words* created the *earthly* environment for vegetation, seed, and fruit.[9] Then God said, "Lights in the dome of the sky," and this *word* separated the light from the darkness.[10] Once light and darkness are separated so they create day and night, God begins to create *life* (*zōē*) in the form of *living beings*. After God creates *living beings* to inhabit the waters, to fly in the air, and to dwell on the earth,[11] God creates humankind in God's own image.[12] According to the *cosmic story of creation* in the gospel of John, this means that *life*, which is *in* both

---

8. Gen 1:3; John 1:9.
9. Gen 1:3–13; cf. John 1:3, 10.
10. Gen 1:14–19; cf. John 1:5.
11. Gen 1:20–25; cf. John 1:4.
12. Gen 1:26–27.

the Father and the *word* (*logos*), *flows* through *the word* into the created world. The *words* God spoke created *living beings* to swim in the sea, to fly in the air, and to live on the earth, because *life* was *in the words God spoke*. According to the Johannine version of creation, God's *word* (*logos*) *is the divine agent and agency that gives life,* because the Word *has* life *in him*.[13] And this takes us back to John 3:16, where because God *loves* the world God *gave* his only Son (the *logos* of God who *has life in him*), so that those who believe in him may not perish but *have* everlasting *life*. What God *gives* through his *word* is *life* rather than *love* in the gospel of John. In Paul's letters, the Spirit *pours love* into the hearts of humans; in John, the Spirit *gives everlasting life* to those who *believe* in the Son.

This takes us to words at the end of chapter 3 in John, which introduce readers to more of *the Johannine cosmic story*:

> He whom God has sent speaks *the words of God*, for he *gives* the Spirit without measure. The Father *loves* (*agapāi*) the Son and has *given* all things into his hands. Whoever believes in the Son *has* everlasting life; whoever disobeys the Son will *not see life*.[14]

In John the words of Logos Jesus *give* the Spirit in abundance to humans. The Spirit *interprets* the words of Logos Jesus, teaching believers "everything" and reminding them of all that Logos Jesus said to them.[15] Among these words are the statements that the Father *loves* the Son and *has given all things into his hands,* and whoever believes in the Son *has* everlasting life and whoever disobeys the Son will not see *life*. Why this emphasis on those who disobey *not* seeing life? Why not simply emphasize that those who *love* the Son *receive* life?

Throughout the gospel of John readers hear many *negative* statements. Why so? Why not simply talk positively about love, light, and life? The first reason is that the storyline of John gives hearers an experience of light coming through darkness into the hearts, minds, and souls of believers. The prologue to John asserts that "The true light, which enlightens everyone, was coming into the world."[16] Statements about *love* occur only occasionally throughout the first twelve chapters, and most of the time the context is negative. In chapter five Jesus tells Judeans in Jerusalem: "I know you do

---

13. Since *the word* has masculine gender (*ho logos*), it is natural for *the word* on earth to be *a man* (*anēr*); see John 1:30.

14. John 3:34–36 auth. var.

15. John 14:26.

16. John 1:9.

not have the love of God in you."¹⁷ Then later he says to them, "If God were your Father, you would love me, for I came from God, and now I am here. I did *not* come on my own, but he sent me."¹⁸ The pervading darkness in the hearts of humans creates the overall context for *the Son* to come into the world as *light* which comes through the darkness and overcomes it.

There seems also to be another reason for the negativity that occurs so frequently in the gospel of John. People who taught rhetoric in the Mediterranean world, namely people who taught students how to present a persuasive argument in a public setting, emphasized the importance of embedding negative assertions in positive assertions. One of the most well-known examples of this in our experience is the famous statement of President John F. Kennedy: "Ask *not* what your country can do for you. Ask what you can do for your country." In this statement, the opening negative, "ask *not*," dramatically sets up the assertion that people *should ask* what they *can do* for their country. In the gospel of John, Jesus regularly speaks in this *rhetorical* style.

But there is yet one more thing about the inclusion of negative statements. Interweaving positive and negative statements is a poetic wisdom way of speaking, like we saw in the previous chapter with Paul's statements about *love* in 1 Corinthians 13. Paul's negative statements in the midst of his positive statements about *love* implant the imagery of *love* in the hearts of the hearers as *wisdom*. Statements about *love* in the gospel of John show how God's *love* implants *everlasting life* into the bodies of hearers who *believe*, much like God implanted *wisdom* in King Solomon. The gospel of John, then, participates in the overall movement from Torah commandment to poetic wisdom that speaks about *bringing life* from God to humans on earth.

When Jesus explains his relation to the Father in chapter five of the gospel of John, he begins with a negative statement, "Very truly, I tell you, the Son can do *nothing* on his own." The purpose of this negative statement, of course, is to introduce a string of positive statements:

> But only what he sees the Father doing,
>   for whatever the Father does, the Son does likewise.
> The Father *loves* the Son and shows him all that he himself is doing,
>   and he will show him greater works than these, so that you
>   will be astonished.

17. John 5:42.
18. John 8:42.

> Indeed, just as the Father raises the dead and gives them *life*,
> so also the Son *gives life* to whomever he wishes.[19]

Here we see how the Son imitates the Father in the gospel of John. A son's imitation of his father is a major way in which *wisdom* is handed down through the generations in Jewish Wisdom literature. In the gospel of John, this mode of imitation is built into the relation of the Son to the Father. According to the passage just quoted, the Son's imitation of the Father is a continually ongoing activity. And we must notice that *the* major activity of the Father, and therefore the Son, is *bringing life* into the world. The passage above continues until Jesus introduces a negative statement that prepares the way for a conclusion that intermingles negative with positive statements about *life* and *everlasting life*:

> Anyone who does *not* honor the Son
> does *not* honor the Father who sent him.
> Very truly, I tell you, anyone who hears my *word* (*logon*)
> and believes him who sent me *has* everlasting *life*,
> And does *not* come under judgment,
> but has passed from death to *life*.[20]

Here we see sustained reference to the *flow* of *life* from the Father through the Son into the world. The Father has *sent* the Son *into the cosmos* to *give life*, and this requires the performance of tasks we will explore in just a moment. Before we do, we remind ourselves once more that much of the talk about *love* and *life* in the gospel of John intermingles positive statements with negative assertions, and this is characteristic of poetic wisdom speech. We have seen that references to *love* occur only occasionally in the first twelve chapters of John, and these chapters indicate that *the words* of Logos Jesus *give life* to *those who believe*. In these initial chapters, *love* and *life* are moving through the darkness in the world to bring *life* into the world. So how does the Johannine storyline unfold as it presents its account of the *earthly-cosmic* drama through which *everlasting life* comes from God's *love* to those who believe?

---

19. John 5:19–21.
20. John 5:23–24 auth. var.

Love, Life, and Friendship in the Gospel of John

THE *CHAIN OF LOVE* IN THE SON'S FAREWELL IN JOHN 13–17

Instead of a three-chapter Sermon on the Mount at the beginning of Jesus' ministry, as there is in Matthew 5–7, the gospel of John has a five-chapter Farewell in John 13–17. This is the place in the gospel of John where Jesus does his most extensive teaching about *love*. Jesus' Farewell begins on the night before the festival of Passover, when he gathers with his disciples and washes their feet. The gospel of John opens the chapter in this manner:

> Now before the festival of the Passover, Jesus knew that his hour had come to depart from this world and go to the Father. Having *loved* his own who were in the world, he *loved* them to the end.[21]

We notice here how Jesus focuses on *his own* in relation to his departure to *the Father*. In this context he focuses on his *love* for those who *believe* in him and the necessity for them to *love one another*. After Jesus washes the feet of his disciples to show them an example for their actions of *love*,[22] he tells them:

> I give you a new commandment, that you *love* one another. Just as I have *loved* you, you also should *love* one another. By this everyone will know that you are my disciples, if you have *love* for one another.[23]

Here we see an important step in *the chain of love* that gradually comes into view as the storyline of John unfolds. There are three *reciprocal links* in the Johannine chain of love. The *first link* is the reciprocal love of the Father for the Son and the Son for the Father. This link generates *love* within the Son. The *second link* is the reciprocal love of the Son for *his own*. This link generates *love* within *the Son's own* so they also *love* the Son. Since the *love* within the Son is also the Father's love, those who love the Son also love the Father and the Father loves them. Then there is a *third link*. Those who love the Son and the Father will also *love one another*. In other words, when Jesus says, "Just as I have *loved* you, you also should love one another. By this everyone will know that you are my disciples, if you have *love* for one another," we are to understand that we are seeing how the *third link* involves *us* in the *Johannine chain of love*.

21. John 13:1.
22. John 13:15.
23. John 13:34–35.

Finding Love

And now we must notice the additional thing Jesus said to them. When Jesus is speaking he says he is *giving* them *a new commandment*. At this point we need to know an additional part of the storyline of Wisdom in the wisdom literature that was emerging in Judaism. Both in Sirach and Baruch (see the Greek Old Testament display in the previous chapter) Wisdom is identified as the Torah and the Book of Covenant which God gave to Israel: Sirach says:

> All this [wisdom] is the book of the covenant of the Most High God, the Torah that Moses commanded us as an inheritance for the congregations of Jacob.[24]

Baruch puts it this way:

> Learn where there is wisdom, where there is strength, where there is understanding, so that you may at the same time discern where there is length of days and *life*, where there is *light* for the eyes, and peace... She [Wisdom] is the book of the commandments of God, the Torah that endures forever. All who hold her fast will *live*, and those who forsake her will die.[25]

As we remind ourselves that three of the books that *expanded* the Hebrew Bible into the Greek Old Testament were *wisdom* books (Wisdom of Solomon, Sirach, Baruch), we need to know that the overall effect of these books was to *transform* the Torah (Genesis–Deuteronomy), which included the Book of the Covenant (Exodus 20–23), into *wisdom sayings*. These wisdom sayings regularly were shorter than the commandments in the Torah and the Book of the Covenant, so they could easily be memorized, remembered, and recited. For example, the commandment to love one's neighbor in Leviticus is quite lengthy:

> You shall not go around as a slanderer among your people, but you shall love your neighbor as yourself: I am YHWH.[26]

By the first century CE, this commandment had become simply "Love your neighbor as yourself." This is now a wisdom saying understood as a commandment. We see this process clearly in the New Testament, where all of the commandments are recited in a shortened, wisdom-saying form. It also

---

24. Sir 24:23 auth. var.
25. Bar 3:14; 4:1 auth. var.
26. Lev 19:18 auth. var.

was a process that was occurring in the Wisdom books in the Greek Old Testament.

Jews understood *wisdom*, then, as *transformed commandment*, and we see this process clearly in the gospel of John. While Paul preferred to transform commandments into statements that "*Love* does . . . and *love* does not do . . . ," the gospel of John has Logos Jesus *openly* call his words *commandments* which *those who love him* will keep. The gospel of John considers sayings of Jesus to be *words* of the Father that have been *given* to the Son *to give to* the world for the purpose of *giving* everlasting life to *those who believe* in the Son, *love* the Son, and *keep* his *words* (commandments).

THE *CHAIN OF COMMANDMENT* IN THE GOSPEL OF JOHN

When Jesus refers to a *commandment*, we are seeing a link in the *commandment chain* in the gospel of John that is at work in the *chain of love* from the Father through the Son to *those who love the Son*. Like the *chain of love*, the *chain of commandment* has *three links*. These links are part of the *love-chain*, and they make the chain a *love-commandment chain*. The *first link* in the *chain of commandment* is *ongoing commandments* the Father gives to the Son and the Son's obedience to those commandments. The *chain of commandment* functions in the context of the Father's *love* for the Son and the Son's *love* for the Father. Because of the Son's *love for the Father*, the Son *continually does* what the Father *commands* him to do. In John 14:31, Jesus says, "I do as the Father has *commanded* me, so that the world may know that I *love* the Father." The Father has given *many commandments* to the Son, which the Son obeys. One of the chief commandments the Father gave to the Son was "to lay down his living being and take it up again." As Jesus says,

> For this reason the Father *loves* me: that I lay down my living being so that I may take it up again. No one has taken it from me; rather I lay it down, and I have power to take it up again; this *command* I received from my Father.[27]

As the storyline unfolds, the *second link* in the chain of commandment emerges. This link is that *all the words* the Son has spoken *to his own* are

---

27. John 10:17–18; David Bentley Hart, *The New Testament: A Translation* (2nd ed.; New Haven: Yale University Press, 2023) with auth. var.

commandments to which *those who love him* will be obedient. Jesus explains this in the following way:

> They who have my *commandments* and keep them are those who *love* me, and those who *love* me will be *loved* by my Father, and I will *love* them and manifest myself (*emphanisō*) to them." Judas (not Iscariot) said to him, "Lord, how is it that you will manifest (*emphanizein*) yourself to us, and *not* to the world?" Jesus answered him, "Those who *love* me will *keep my word*, and my Father will *love* them, and we will come to them and make our home with them. Whoever does *not* love me does *not* keep my words (*logous*), and the word (*logos*) that you hear is *not* mine but is from the Father who sent me."[28]

Here we see the *chain of love* explained in relation to *the commandments* the Son has given to his disciples. Then there is the *third link* in the chain of commandment, which is the *new commandment* that *his own* will *love one another* as he has loved them. When they *love one another,* the Son and the Father *will come to them* and *make their home with them*. This leads us to a discussion of *abiding*.

THE *CHAIN OF ABIDING* IN THE GOSPEL OF JOHN

An additional part of the *love-commandment chain* in the gospel of John is a *chain of abiding*, which is a reconfiguration of the *tenting* of Wisdom among the people of Israel. We saw in the previous chapter how God *commanded* Wisdom to go and *make her tent* (*kataskēnōson*) in Israel:

> Then the Creator of all things gave me a *command* (*eneteilato*),
>   and my Creator pitched my tent (*skēnēn*).
>   He said, "Encamp (*kataskēnōson*) in Jacob, and in Israel receive your inheritance."[29]

As mentioned earlier, toward the end of the prologue in John there is an assertion that applies this *tenting* to the Logos become flesh in Jesus Christ:

---

28. John 14:21–24 auth. var.
29. Sir 24:8.

the Word became flesh and *tented* (*eskēnōsen*) among us, and we have seen his glory, the glory as of a father's only son, full of grace and truth.[30]

We also see that Logos Jesus' becoming flesh, laying down his living being, and taking his living being up again is a result of the Son's obedience to a *command* of the Father:

> For this reason the Father loves me, because I lay down my living being in order to take it up again. No one has taken it from me, but I lay it down of my own accord. I have power to lay it down, and I have power to take it up again. I received this *command* from my Father.[31]

When the gospel of John says that *the Word* became flesh and *tented* among us, we must understand that *the Word* was responding to a *command* of the Father for him to do this. When we get to Jesus' Farewell in John 13–17, Jesus refers to this *tenting* as *abiding* (*menein*). This leads to the *chain of abiding* that is present in the *love-commandment chain*. Again there are *three links*. The *first link* is that the Father abides in the Son and the Son abides in the Father. The *second link* is that the Son abides in his own, which also means that *the Father and the Son* make their *home* (*monēn*) in *those who keep his word* (14:23). Then Jesus explains that the *third link* in the *chain of abiding* is that his own *bear much* fruit. Jesus says it in this way:

> Abide in me as I abide in you. Just as the branch cannot bear fruit by itself unless it abides in the vine, neither can you unless you abide in me. I am the vine, you are the branches. Those who abide in me and I in them bear much fruit, because apart from me you can do nothing.[32]

Then Jesus explains the presence of the Father in all of this:

> As the Father has *loved* me, so I have *loved* you; *abide* (*meinate*) in my *love*. If you keep my commandments, you will *abide* (*meneite*) in my *love*, just as I have kept my Father's commandments and *abide* (*menō*) in his *love*.[33]

---

30. John 1:14 auth. var.
31. John 10:17–18 auth. var.
32. John 15:4–5.
33. John 15:9–10.

Here we see in the gospel of John the reconfiguration of the full circle of the Jewish story of Wisdom. While Wisdom was present with God at creation in the Jewish Wisdom storyline, the Word (*logos*) is not only present with God at creation in the gospel of John but also is *the agent and agency* through whom the world is created and *life* comes into the world. As Wisdom traveled through the cosmos until God commanded her to come to earth and *tent* among the people of Israel, so Logos Jesus, responding to a command of the Father, came to earth and *tented* among *his own* who had been created through him. As the gospel of John reconfigures the Jewish Wisdom storyline in relation to the life, death, and exaltation of Jesus, there is promise that both the Father and the Son will come and *abide* in those who *keep* the words of Logos Jesus. For the gospel of John, this means that those who *keep* the words of Logos Jesus will *abide* in the *love* of Logos Jesus, and just as the Son *abides* in the Father's *love* so will those who love the Son abide in the Father's love. And, reciprocally, the Father and the Son will abide in those who *love the Son*. The end result of the Jewish story of Wisdom is the enjoyment of a full life through obedience to God's commandments. The gospel of John reconfigures this into a life that bears the fruit of *loving one another*, which leads to joy being complete in all who live in this love.

BECOMING A FRIEND (*PHILOS*) OF LOGOS JESUS IN THE GOSPEL OF JOHN

Perhaps one of the most surprising things in the gospel of John is movement of Jesus' discussion of *love* to a point where he calls his disciples *friends*. Let us recall that in the first chapter of this book we noticed how God spoke to Moses *as a friend* when he told him all the commandments of the Book of the Covenant. We noticed in that context and in the chapter on *love* in Paul how Stephen Fowl expanded this relation between God and Moses into an assertion that God's giving of scripture to believers is a major way in which God invites humans to become *friends* of God.

In the middle of Jesus' Farewell in the Gospel of John, Jesus reinterprets the commandment to love one another into a statement about his relation to his disciples as *friends*:

> This is my commandment, that you love one another as I have loved you. No one has greater love than this, to lay down one's living being for one's *friends* (*philōn*). You are my *friends* (*philoi*) if

you do what I command you. I do not call you *slaves* (*doulous*) any longer, because the *slave* (*doulos*) does not know what the master is doing, but I have called you *friends* (*philous*), *because I have made known to you everything that I have heard from my Father.*[34]

With this teaching, Logos Jesus is reshaping the *friendship* God established with Moses when he told Moses *all* the commandments it was necessary for the people of Israel to do to have life filled with the blessings of the covenant. In the gospel of John, Logos Jesus says he has *made known* to his disciples *everything he has heard from his Father*. In essence, *everything the Father has told the Son* is *scripture*, namely *word of God*. The gospel of John as we hear it presents what Logos Jesus spoke to his disciples *in written form*. The gospel of John, then, is presenting *the Father's words*, spoken by Logos Jesus, as *scripture* (written *scripted words of God*). In other words, Logos Jesus has spoken *intimately* to his disciples, telling them *everything the Father has told him*. And this is what *friends* do. They *tell each other everything*, and they are willing *to lay their living being down* for their friends.

When Jesus reaches the point of *friendship* with his disciples, he is *explicitly* moving beyond language in the synoptic gospels. In the gospel of Mark, Jesus tells Peter, James, John, and Andrew *everything before the end comes*.[35] But he cannot tell them *the day* or *the hour* of the end, because *no one knows, not even the angels in heaven, nor the Son, but only the Father*.[36] In the synoptic gospels, the Son *does not know everything the Father knows*. But in the gospel of John, the Father and the Son have such an intimate relation that the Son *knows the whole story* of what the Father is doing. The Son keeps watching and listening continually to see what the Father is doing and to hear what the Father is saying. Then the Son *imitates* what the Father does and *tells* those who love him what the Father *says*.

As a result of this especially intimate relation between the Father and the Son in the gospel of John, Jesus' relation to his disciples becomes one of *friends*. This is an explicit reworking of Jesus' relation to his disciples in the synoptic gospels. In Mark and Matthew, Jesus teaches his disciples that the Son of Man did not come to be served but to serve. Then he uses the language of servant-slave (*diakonos-doulos*) to say:

> You know that among the gentiles those whom they recognize as their rulers lord it over them, and their great ones are tyrants

---

34. John 15:12–15 auth. var.
35. Mark 13:23.
36. Mark 13:32, 35; Matt 24:36; 25:13.

Finding Love

> over them. But it is not so among you; instead, whoever wishes to become great among you must be your *servant* (*diakonos*), and whoever wishes to be first among you must be *slave* (*doulos*) of all. For the Son of Man came not to be served but to serve and to give his life a ransom for many.[37]

In Mark and Matthew, Jesus explicitly uses the term *slave* to describe and explain the relation of his disciples to those among whom they live. In John, Jesus *explicitly* moves *beyond* imagery of being a *slave* to being a *friend*. No one has greater *love* than this, to *lay down one's living being* for one's *friends*. Logos Jesus *no longer* calls his disciples *slaves*, because slaves *do not know what the master is doing*. Logos Jesus has made everything known to them that *he heard from the Father*. Therefore, they *know* and *understand* what he is doing. This makes them *friends*.

By analogy, Moses became a friend of God when God told him the Torah and the Book of Covenant which *made known to Moses* all the things God was doing. Now the gospel of John is reshaping this *friendship* with God through Logos Jesus, who has told them *all the things* the Father has told him. Rather than giving *new Torah*, as Jesus does in the gospel of Matthew, Logos Jesus gives *the words of God* that the Son has received from the Father. These *words* are *commandments*, and those who *keep* these commandments become *friends* of Logos Jesus. Jesus concludes his statements with:

> You did not choose me, but I chose you. And I appointed you to go and bear fruit, fruit that will last, so that the Father will give you whatever you ask him in my name. I am giving you these *commands* so that you may *love one another*.[38]

Just as God chose Israel and sent Wisdom to go and *tent* among them, in the gospel of John Logos Jesus chooses disciples, abides in them, and appoints them to go and bear fruit that will last as they *love one another*. In this context, they are *friends* of the Son, and they will be willing *to lay down their living being* for *their friends*.

---

37. Mark 10:42–45; cf. Matt 20:27; Luke 22:26.
38. John 15:16–17.

Love, Life, and Friendship in the Gospel of John

CONCLUSION

We have now reached a highpoint in our journey together finding love in the Bible. In the gospel of John we *clearly* see God's *love* for the world. We also see the Father's love for the Son, the Son's *love* for the Father, and the Son's *love* for those who *love* him. We have arrived here through a journey with Wisdom in emerging *wisdom literature* within Judaism during the time of the emergence of Christianity.

In this chapter we have come to understand *wisdom* as *transformed commandment*. We have learned that Jews, living in the Hellenistic world where Greek philosophy was flourishing, were transforming the Torah and the Book of the Covenant into poetic wisdom sayings. We saw in the previous chapter how Paul not only interpreted *Christ* Jesus as God's wisdom, but he interpreted *love* as *wisdom poured* into the hearts of believers by the Holy Spirit so they would *love one another*. In this context, Paul transformed commandments into statements of what "*Love* does . . . and *love* does not do . . . ." In other words, Paul personified *love* as an *acting agent* within believers, enabling them to live a life of love. The gospel of John takes a step further into the world of Jewish wisdom by calling the *sayings* of Logos Jesus *commandments* which those who *love* the Son will keep.

We have seen in this chapter that the gospel of John reshapes the story of Wisdom in Jewish literature into *a cosmic story* of the Father and the Son. The Son sees what the Father is doing and does likewise. Also, the Son hears what the Father is saying and tells those who love him what the Father has spoken to him. In this context, Logos Jesus *openly* calls God's words and his own words *commandments* which *those who love him* will keep. A major reason the sayings of Jesus in the gospel of John are considered to be *commandments* is that *the words* the Son has spoken are *words* the Father has *given* to the Son *to give to* the world. This chain of transmission of the words of God occur in a *love-commandment-abiding chain* whereby *everlasting life is given* to *those who believe* in the Son, *love* the Son, and *keep* his commandments (words).

So, we see that the overall message in the gospel of John is *the cosmic story* of the Father's *sending* of Jesus into the world to present the Father's *word*. This is what makes John so different from the synoptic gospels. After the Son speaks the Father's *word* on earth, the Son departs to be with the Father and both the Father and the Son *come to* those who keep Jesus' *word* and "make their home in them." This will happen because, as Logos Jesus says, "Those who *love* me will keep *my word*, and my Father will *love* them."[39] This is so different from the synoptic gospels, where the disciples are told to look for the coming of the Son of Man in clouds with great power and glory.[40] In John, if the disciples obey the Son's word, both the Father and the Son will abide in their *love*.

QUESTIONS FOR DISCUSSION

1. What is a key difference between the Jewish Shema and John 3:16? In other words, which way does love flow in the Jewish Shema? Which way does love flow in John 3:16?

2. How does creation occur in Genesis 1 so that it is open to an *interpretation* that *Word* creates? How is it possible to interpret Genesis 1 so that *Word* has *life* in it?

3. *Love* appears only occasionally during the first twelve chapters of John. According to the author of this book on *Finding Love*, this is because of the darkness in this world. What is the relation of *love* to *light* in the gospel of John so that *love* only gradually becomes a major topic of conversation?

4. *Love* becomes a major topic of conversation in John 13–17. What is happening in those chapters that makes a discussion of *love* so important?

5. *Love* becomes a *chain of love* in John 13–17. There are *three links* in this *chain of love*. Can you explain what makes each link in the chain a *link*? In other words, what does a *link* look like, so that a *link* is a good image for each part of *the chain*?

6. In John 13–17 a *chain of commandment* emerges from the Father to those who love the Son. There are *three links* in this chain that is embedded in the *chain of love*. Can you describe each link in the *chain of commandment* and describe how each link functions in the *chain of love*?

7. In John 13–17 a *chain of abiding* emerges in the *love-commandment* chain. Can you describe the *chain of abiding*? What is the relation of the *chain of abiding* in the gospel of John to the *tenting* in Jewish wisdom literature?

---

39. John 14:23.
40. Mark 13:26; cf. Matt 24:30; Luke 21:27.

8. In John 15 Jesus tells his disciples they are his *friends*. How is this a reconfiguration of God's spending time *face to face* with Moses on Mount Sinai when God spoke the commandments and the Book of Covenant to Moses?

9. What are the two major characteristics of *friends* in the Gospel of John? How do these two characteristics differ from the way in which God and Moses were *friends*? How are these two characteristics similar to the way in which God and Moses were *friends*?

10. In the beginning part of this chapter it was asserted that *belief* in the gospel of John was focused on *believing a cosmic story*. Can you tell this *cosmic story*? How many parts would you say there are to this *cosmic story*?

11. What is the special title for God in the Johannine *cosmic story*? What is the special title for Jesus in this *cosmic story*? Why does the focus of *belief* have to be on a *cosmic story* rather than simply or primarily on God or on Jesus in the gospel of John?

6

Cosmic Peace, Church, and Love in Colossians

> I want their hearts to be encouraged and united in love,
> so that they may have all the riches of assured understanding
> and have the knowledge of God's mystery, that is, Christ himself.[1]

IN THE PREVIOUS CHAPTER we saw how the gospel of John brings *love* to its fullest expression among the gospels. John does this by presenting *a cosmic story* about the Father's *love* that *tents* on earth through the speech (*logos*) and activity of the Son. The cosmic story begins with an interpretation of creation in Genesis that emphasizes *life* coming into the cosmos, and this focus on *life* moves into a discussion of belief that brings *everlasting life* into humans.

In this chapter we see how Colossians brings *love* to a fuller expression in the letters of Paul. To be sure, many of the most treasured Pauline passages on love are in 1 Corinthians, Romans, and Philippians. In this chapter we will see that Colossians creates *cosmic picturing* rather than *cosmic storytelling* to show how *love fills* the cosmos with abundant, ever-growing, ever-flourishing fruitfulness of blessing.

As we proceed, we will see how Colossians transforms statements in early letters of Paul into statements that present *cosmic picturing*. We will see four ways in which the wording in Colossians does this:

---

1. Col 2:2 NRSV.

1. Rephrasing clauses and sentences in Paul's early letters;
2. Filling *love* with wisdom, understanding, and full knowledge;
3. Using the word-stem or word for *fullness* (*plēro-, plērōma*) and *all* (*pan, pas-*) or *everything* (*panta*) to describe God's love;
4. Creating more complex verbs to describe the relation of believers to Christ.

These changes seem to have come into Colossians through *writing activity* by scribes who were familiar with Paul's earlier letters, rather than by *oral dictation* of these letters by Paul himself. This document presents important developments of theological and practical thinking that move beyond what is observed in earlier letters of Paul. As a result, the sentences in Colossians are longer than sentences in Paul's early letters. Often, then, a person may find them more difficult to *read aloud* to an audience than Paul's early letters. So bear with me dear readers as we continue our journey, even if it seems complex.

THE PAULINE *COSMIC PICTURE* OF GOD'S LOVE

A Pauline *interpretation* of creation is present in Colossians 1:15–20. Interpreters regularly refer to these verses either as *the Colossians hymn* or *the Christ hymn* in Colossians. All interpreters agree that these verses are poetic, and most interpreters think they probably existed as a self-contained statement within early church liturgy. Some interpreters think it is a misunderstanding to say these verses are a hymn, because there is no clear evidence they were *sung*. These poetic verses rewrite Genesis 1 in a manner related to the opening verses in John. But rather than telling a *cosmic story*, the poetic verses in Colossians *picture* the creation by declaring that *the Son of God's love*[2] is the *image* of the unseen (*aoratou*) God, the *firstborn* (*prototokos*) of all creation (*pasēs ktiseōs*). While we did not mention it earlier, the prologue in the gospel of John ends with an assertion that "no one has ever seen God."[3] Then it continues by saying that the *only-begotten* (*monogenēs*), "who is in the bosom of the Father has made him known."[4] In

---

2. Col 1:13: *tou huios tēs agapēs autou*.
3. John 1:18.
4. John 1:18 says the *only-begotten* has "exegeted (*exegēsato*) God," the technical term scholars use to *interpret* Scripture.

other words, when the Logos becomes flesh and *tents* among humans, people are able to see the works and hear the sayings of the Father. Colossians agrees that humans are not able to see God directly. They can only see *imagery* of God in God's Son *Christ* Jesus.

The Colossians verses focus on *seeing* without an equal focus on *hearing* as they use the word *image* (*eikōn*) to describe the relation of the Son to the Father. For Colossians, humans can see the *image* of the Father through *the Son of his love*. Here the Colossians verses are reconfiguring Wisdom of Solomon which states that:

> She (wisdom) is a reflection of everlasting light,
>   a spotless mirror of the *energy* (*energeias*) of God,
>   and an *image* (*eikon*) of his goodness.[5]

As the Colossians verses unfold, they describe the Son as *protos* (first) rather than *mono* (only), as the gospel of John does.[6] This emphasis on *first* is a reconfiguration of Proverbs:

> The Lord created me (*wisdom*) in the beginning (*archēn*) as the ways of his works,
>   He established me as the foundation in the beginning (*archēi*)
> before (*pro*) the ages,
> before (*pro*) he made the earth
>   and before (*pro*) he made the depths,
> before (*pro*) the springs of the waters came forth,
>   before (*pro*) the mountains had been shaped,
> before (*pro*) all the hills he brought me forth.[7]

The Colossians hymn reconfigures the function of Wisdom in Proverbs into *Christ,* the Son of God's love who is:

> firstborn (*prōtotokos*) of all creation, . . .
>
> before (*pro*) all things, . . .
>
> the beginning (*archē*), firstborn (*prōtotokos*) out of the dead,
>
> so that he might become himself first (*prōteuōn*) in all things (*pasin*).[8]

---

5. Wis 7:26 auth. trans.

6. No letter attributed to Paul ever uses the term *monogenēs* (only-begotten).

7. Prov 8:22–25 LXX auth. trans.

8. Col 1:15, 17–18; trans. Roy R. Jeal, *Exploring Colossians: Living the New Reality* (Rhetoric of Religious Antiquity 5; Atlanta: SBL Press, 2024) 91.

Cosmic Peace, Church, and Love in Colossians

In Colossians, the Son is the *firstborn* who "created all things in the heavens and on the earth, the *seen* and the *unseen* things."[9] Then the hymn says, "all things (*panta*) have been created *through* him and *for* him; and he is *before* (*pro*) all things, and all things hold together *in him*."[10] Here we get a first glimpse of how Colossians reconfigures the story of Jewish Wisdom both during creation and as she traveled through *all the cosmos* before coming to *tent* on earth.

In Colossians, the Son *Christ* Jesus is the *cosmic energy* (*energeia*) of all things seen and unseen. Colossians does not emphasize that this cosmic energy is *life* (*zōē*) in the same way the gospel of John does. Rather, the focus of the Pauline hymn is on *cosmic energy* of the Son both on earth and throughout the cosmos that *creates peace* (*eirēnē*). The Son reconciles *"all things to himself,* making peace through the blood of his cross, *whether things on the earth, whether things in the heavens."*[11] In other words, rather than the Son *laying down his living being and taking it up again*, as in John, the Pauline emphasis is on the Son as *creator of peace* throughout all the cosmos. Colossians describes this activity of the Son as bringing *the fullness* (*plērōma*) of God into the entire cosmos, because "in him all the *fullness* was pleased to *house* (*katoikēsai*)."[12]

Here we see Colossians changing *tenting* (*kataskēnōsai*) on earth to *housing* (*katoikēsai*). The underlying Greek word in Colossians is *oikos*, house, rather than *skēnos* or *skēnē*, tent. When Paul talks about *building up* the community in his letters the Greek verb is *oikodomein*, which literally means to *build a house with a dome* on it. For Paul, God's love *houses* on earth rather than *tents* on earth. This still follows the story of Jewish Wisdom, because within time Wisdom moved beyond *tenting*, moving from place to place in the tabernacle, to *housing* in the Jerusalem temple. Sirach has Wisdom explain it like this:

> Before (*pro*) the ages, in the beginning, he (God) created me,
>   and for all the ages I shall not cease to be.
> In the holy tent (*skēnēi*) I ministered before him,
>   and so I was established in Zion.
> Thus in the beloved (*ēgapēmenēi*) city (*polei*) he gave me a resting place,
>   and in Jerusalem was my domain.[13]

---

9. Col 1:16; trans. Jeal, *Exploring Colossians*, 91.
10. Col 1:16–17; trans. Jeal, *Exploring Colossians*, 91.
11. Col 1:20; trans. Jeal, *Exploring Colossians*, 91.
12. Col 1:19; trans. Jeal, *Exploring Colossians*, 91.
13. Sir 24:9–11.

Finding Love

After *tenting* regularly in the tabernacle as Israel traveled from Mount Sinai to Israel, Wisdom finally *housed herself* in the Jerusalem temple that Solomon built. For Colossians *the Son of God's love houses* in the cosmos itself, rather than in Jerusalem. As Colossians says, "he is *before* all things, and *all things (ta panta)* hold together *(synestēken) in him*."[14] Here we see the *cosmic* scope of the *picture* of the Son in Colossians. This is a reconfiguration of the Wisdom of Solomon where it states:

> The spirit of the Lord has *filled (peplērōken)* the world
> and that which *holds all things together (synechon ta panta)* knows what is said.[15]

For Colossians, the Son of God's *love* contains both wisdom and Spirit so that "he is before all things, and all things hold together in him."[16] So the Son is not limited to the temple in Jerusalem. But even this was prepared for by the history of Israel, when the Jerusalem temple was made unholy through actions of Greek rulers who entered it and desecrated it. In this context, a book not in the Greek Old Testament but present among the Qumran Dead Sea writings and in the Ethiopian Old Testament, asserts:

> Wisdom did not find a place where she might dwell,
>   so her dwelling was in the heavens.
> Wisdom went forth to dwell among the sons of men,
>   but she did not find a dwelling.
> Wisdom returned to her place,
>   and sat down in the midst of the angels.[17]

Within Israel itself there came a time when the Jerusalem temple was so defiled that Wisdom went back into the heavens and dwelt among the angels. Colossians extends this Enochian view of Wisdom's journey by having the Son *housed above* with God where the Son is *the head* of the body, the church *(ekklēsia)*, which extends through the heavens down to the earth. As the Colossians hymn states it:

> he [the Son] is the head of the body, the *ekklēsia*, who is the beginning, *firstborn (prototokos)* out of the dead, so that he might become himself first *(proteuōn)* in all things, because in him all the

---

14. Col 1:17; trans. Jeal, *Exploring Colossians*, 91; cf. Sir 1:7.
15. Wis 1:7.
16. Col 1:17; trans. Jeal, *Exploring Colossians*, 91.
17. 1 Enoch 42:1–2; trans. George W. E. Nickelsburg and James VanderKam, *1 Enoch 2* (Hermeneia; Minneapolis: Fortress, 2012) 138.

fullness (*plērōma*) was pleased to *house* (*katoikēsai*), and through him to reconcile all things (*ta panta*) to himself, making peace (*eirēnopoiēsas*) through the blood of his cross, whether things on the earth, whether things in the heavens.[18]

We see in Colossians, therefore, how the Pauline *cosmic picture* envisions the Son and the Father *abiding above,* but the *church* is a *cosmic church* (*ekklēsia*) that extends from *above* down onto the earth. A major dimension of this church is the *peace energy* that *houses* in it. This *peace energy* was active in the exaltation of *Christ above* after his crucifixion. As a result, this *peace energy* exists not only in the church on earth but extends upward and outward throughout the entire cosmos. As the Son *houses in the cosmos,* he is the head of the church (*ekklēssia*). In the previous chapter on the gospel of John we saw how *love flows* from *above to the earth* through the Son so that the Father and the Son *come and abide in believers.* In Colossians, the sphere of love and light that exists *above extends down on the earth* through *the church, the body of Christ.* How can this happen?

BEING *MADE ALIVE* WITH *CHRIST*

For Colossians, the kingdom of God is not *coming to earth,* as in the synoptic gospels. Also, believers do not simply *receive* love, life, peace, joy, and the Holy Spirit. Rather, believers already have been transferred into the *kingdom* of the Son of God's love and light[19] through Christ's death and resurrection. This means that believers *already receive* the *cosmic activity* (*energeia*) of God's *love* through *Christ* Jesus, who is the firstborn out of the dead and head of the church. What is the process by which this occurs?

Paul's argument about belief in God's resurrection of *Christ* in 1 Corinthians 15 prepares the way for the view in Colossians. In 1 Corinthians, Paul argues that "as all die in Adam, so all *will be made alive* (*zōipoiēthēsontai*) in Christ."[20] As "the last Adam," *Christ* "became a *life-making* (*zōopoioun*) spirit."[21] Then Paul states:

> The first man was from the earth, made of dust; the second man is from heaven (*ouranou*). As one of dust, so are those who are of

---

18. Col 1:18–20; trans. Jeal, *Exploring Colossians,* 91.
19. Col 1:13.
20. 1 Cor 15:22.
21. 1 Cor 15:45.

the dust, and as one of heaven (*epouranios*), so are those who are of heaven (*epouranioi*). Just as we have borne the image (*eikona*) of the one of dust, we will also bear the image (*eikona*) of the one of heaven.[22]

Colossians expands this statement into a process of re-creation that uses imagery of taking off of old clothes and putting on of new clothes:

> you have taken off the clothes (*apekdusamenoi*) of the old person with its practices and have put on the clothes (*endusamenoi*) of the new person (*ton neon*), which is being renewed (*anakainoumenon*) in full knowledge (*epignōsin*) according to the *image* (*eikona*) of its creator. In that renewal there is no longer Greek and Jew, circumcised and uncircumcised, barbarian, Scythian, slave and free; but *Christ* all and in all (*panta kai en pasin*)![23]

This account of the renewal emphasizes movement beyond *the old person* with its *fleshly* practices toward living in the *full knowledge* of Christ, who is the *image* of God.

In addition to the use of clothing imagery, Colossians reformulates the argumentation so that God's *cosmic activity* (*energeias*) working through the *resurrection of Christ* enacts a *stripping off of the flesh* understood as *non-handmade circumcision*. The *stripping off of the flesh* through *being raised with Christ* is like the resurrection of the dead where what "is sown a physical body...is raised a spiritual body."[24] For this to occur, "this perishable body must *put on* (*endusasthai*) imperishability, and this mortal body must put on (*endusētai*) immortality."[25] Colossians envisions this as having been *raised together* with Christ in God's *cosmic activity* (*energeias*) of non-handmade circumcision, forgiveness of trespasses, and shaming of authorities and powers through *Christ's* crucifixion, burial, and resurrection. This creates a complex picture in which believers are *alive together with Christ*. Colossians explains it in this way:

> in him [*Christ*] *houses* (*katoikei*) all (*pan*) *the fullness* (*plērōma*) of *the deity* (*theotētos*) bodily, and you *have been made full* (*peplērōmenoi*) in him who is the head of every power and authority. In him also you were circumcised with a non-handmade circumcision in the stripping off of the body of the flesh in the

22. 1 Cor 15:47–49.
23. Col 3:9–11 auth. trans.
24. 1 Cor 15:44 auth. trans.
25. 1 Cor 15:53.

> circumcision of Christ, *buried with* (*syntaphentes*) him in baptism in whom also you were *raised* (*synēgerthēte*) through the trustworthy *cosmic activity* (*energeias*) of God who raised him out of [the] dead; and you, being dead in the trespasses and the foreskin of your flesh, he *made you alive with* (*synezōopoiēsen*) him, forgiving us *all* (*panta*) the trespasses, erasing the handwritten record of demands which is opposed to us, and he [himself] took it out of the middle, nailing it to the cross; stripping himself, he disgraced the powers and the authorities in boldness, triumphing them in him.[26]

To communicate the meaning of *being alive with Christ*, Colossians expands the view of being *made alive with Christ* so that the *cosmic energy* of the Son of God's love *is continually active* within believers. Since *circumcision* was such a dramatic marker of membership within God's covenant community, Colossians views believers as *circumcised* with a circumcision *not made with hands* when God raised Christ out of death. As Roy R. Jeal explains it, this means that as believers recall their *baptism* they envision

> "the stripping off of the body of the flesh" [that]...is not the physical flesh of the foreskin but the metaphorical cutting away of the life in darkness and the transfer into the Son's kingdom. The former life has been stripped away and the life of fullness in Christ is now visible and practiced. This is "the circumcision of Christ" (*tēi peritomēi tou Christou*) brought about by the apocalyptic work of God in the death of Christ. It is the action of redemption, forgiveness, reconciliation, and peacemaking that re-envisions what was set in the imagination in 1:12–15.[27]

In other words, as the *cosmic energy* of God raised Christ out of death by transferring him from an earthly body to a cosmic body, so God's action works through *Christ's* resurrection to *strip off the body of flesh* of believers. Believers in the community remember this action in their baptism. God *energizes* their memory by *making the believer alive with Christ*. An important part of the *newness* that occurs through God's action is the removal of *all* the trespasses of believers. Here the wording pictures erasure of the handwritten record of wrongdoing by *taking it out of the middle* and *nailing it to the cross*. The action of nailing the handwritten record to the cross takes away the power of the rulers and authorities who crucified Jesus. This seems to be an expansion of Paul's description of the crucifixion in Galatians:

---

26. Col 2:9–14; trans. Jeal, *Exploring Colossians* 152, 165–66, auth. var.
27. Jeal, *Exploring Colossians*, 161.

> It was before your eyes that Jesus *Christ* was publicly exhibited as crucified![28]

The *nailing to the cross* in Colossians erases the wrongdoing of believers by *taking the record of it out of the middle* and nailing it to the cross. Then the picturing envisions a *parade of triumph,* which often occurred after a Roman military victory. The triumphal parade after the crucifixion makes a public example of the *unclothed* powers and authorities who had previously been dominant. From this perspective, those who previously were powers and authorities are now marching naked and in chains as captured victims in a triumphal parade. The scribes of the letter of Colossians created a special Greek verb to describe this entire process as *being created alive with Christ.*[29] The verb was created with the preposition *with* (*syn*) at the beginning to supplement *to be alive* (*zōi*) and *to create* (*epoiēsen*), which are in the verb in 1 Corinthians 15.[30] This makes *synezōopoiēsen,* which means *to be created alive with.* Then they added *syn autōi* (with him [*Christ*]) in a prepositional phrase after the verb.

Colossians pictures Paul as filled with *Christ's re-creation energy* as he proclaims God's wisdom to the believers in Colossae:

> It is he [*Christ*] whom we proclaim, warning everyone and teaching everyone in all *wisdom* (*sophiāi*), so that we may present everyone *mature* (*teleios*) in *Christ.* For this I toil and struggle with all the *cosmic energy* (*energeian*) that he powerfully *energizes* (*energoumenēn*) within me.[31]

Here we see once again the influence of the cosmic story of Wisdom in Jewish literature of the time. The *cosmic energy* of *wisdom* has become the *re-creation energy* of *Christ's* resurrection that is *alive* within believers and that continually flows through the cosmos, reconciling all opposing powers to one another and creating peace throughout the universe. This leads to Paul's prayer for the people whom he is addressing:

> I want their hearts to be encouraged and united in *love* (*agapēi*) so that they may have *all* (*pan*) the *riches* (*ploutos*) of *full-bearing* (*plērophorias*) understanding and have *full knowledge* (*epignōsin*) of God's mystery, that is, Christ himself, in whom are hidden *all*

---

28. Gal 3:1.
29. Col 2:13; cf. Eph 2:5: *synezōopoiēsen.*
30. 1 Cor 15:22, 36, 45; cf. Rom 4:17; 8:11; 2 Cor 3:6; Gal 3:21; 1 Pet 3:18.
31. Col 1:28–29 auth. trans.

(*pantes*) the *treasures* (*thēsauroi*) of *wisdom* (*sophias*) and *knowledge* (*gnōseōs*).[32]

Here we notice how *love* unites *everything* together. Thus, there is emphasis throughout on *all* the riches and *all* the treasures of understanding, wisdom, and knowledge. In Colossians, the *richness* of God's love comes to believers in *the church* (*ekklēsia*), which is the *cosmic bodily* presence of *Christ* on earth. This *richness* is the *fullness* of God which is provided for believers at all times.

CONCLUSION

As we conclude this chapter it will be good to reflect back on our journey with Paul's letters. We started in 1 Corinthians with *wisdom* becoming *personified love*. There we observed how Paul *fills* love with actions that *build up* the church. *Love*, therefore, does not cause quarrels, disputes, and disagreements but is patient and kind. Colossians takes Paul's concept of *love* much further. Colossians *fills* love with the *richness* of God's *wisdom* and *truth*, which extends far beyond avoiding quarrels into *being made alive with Christ* through the re-creating *cosmic energy* (*energeia*) that is in both God and *Christ*. Colossians *fills love* with wisdom, knowledge, and understanding in this way:

> I want their hearts to be encouraged and united *in love* (*agapēi*), so that they may have all the riches of assured understanding and have the *full knowledge* (*epignōsis*) of God's *mystery* (*mystēriou*), that is, Christ himself, in whom are hidden all the treasures of *wisdom* (*sophias*) and *knowledge*.[33]

---

32. Col 2:2–3 auth. trans.
33. Col 2:2–3 auth. trans.

FINDING LOVE

QUESTIONS FOR DISCUSSION

1. Do you envision worship as bringing you into the presence of God's *cosmic church* with Christ as *the head of the church*?

2. Do you experience God's reconciling all things to himself, creating peace in you and between you and others, as you participate in church?

3. Do you experience God's love as wisdom *tenting* or *housing* in you? If so, explain. If not, explain.

4. Do you experience God's love *making you alive together* with *Christ*? Explain.

5. Are you offended by the idea that God's love *circumcises you* with a circumcision not made with hands? Or are you okay with this imagery?

6. Can you envision God's love as *taking off* the clothes of your flesh and *re-creating you* as a person *clothed* with Christ? Does this imagery work for you? Is this imagery problematic for you? Explain.

7. Does the imagery of God's love *nailing* wrongdoings *to the cross* as an action that *sets aside your wrongdoings* have any meaning for you? Do you like this imagery? Do you not like this imagery? Explain.

7

Cosmic Church, Love, and Mystery in Ephesians

> Be imitators of God, as beloved children,
> and walk in love, as Christ loved us and gave himself up for us,
> a fragrant offering and sacrifice to God.[1]

IN THE PREVIOUS CHAPTER we saw how Colossians transformed statements in early letters of Paul into statements that present *cosmic picturing*. In Colossians, we saw five ways in which the wording in Colossians does this:

1. Rephrasing clauses and sentences in Paul's early letters;

2. Changing *tent* language associated with the Jewish tabernacle into *house* language;

3. Filling *love* with wisdom, understanding, and full knowledge;

4. Using the word-stem or word for *fullness* (*plēro-, plērōma*) and *all* (*pan, pas-*) or *everything* (*panta*) to describe God's love;

5. Creating more complex verbs to describe the relation of believers to *Christ*.

---

1. Eph 5:1–2.

FINDING LOVE

As we move to Ephesians in this chapter, we see four ways Ephesians transforms statements in early letters of Paul into statements that build on the *cosmic picturing* in Colossians:

1. Ephesians changes *house* language into language associated with the Jerusalem temple;
2. Ephesians focuses on the unity of Jews and gentiles in Christ's Church;
3. Ephesians thoroughly embeds the cosmic story of Jewish Wisdom into *Pauline* theology about God's love;
4. Ephesians moves beyond God's love in the Jerusalem temple into God's love in the Church, which God bathes like a husband bathes his wife.

These changes transform the expanded Jewish Shema, where people *love God* and *love their neighbors as themselves,* into a cosmic picture of God's church, where people *love Christ* and *God's church as themselves.*

GOD'S LOVE HAS CREATED ONE NEW HUMANITY IN *CHRIST'S* CHURCH

In Paul's letters *love* unites all the *cosmic activity* of God and *Christ* together into a *cosmic picture* of re-creation of believers through a blending of God's apocalyptic action and baptism. Ephesians builds on the richness of God's love in previous letters to present *a cosmic picture* of the reach of *Christ's church* into both heavenly and earthly spaces and places. First, as Ephesians talks about the richness of God's love it expands *being raised together* with Christ and *being made alive with* Christ with *being seated with* Christ in the heavens. Ephesians presents it like this:

> God, who is *rich (plousios)* in *mercy (eleei),* out of the *great love (pollēn agapēn)* with which he *loved (ēgapēsen)* us even when we were dead through our trespasses, *made us alive with (synezōopoiēsen) Christ*—by grace *(chariti)* you have been saved— and *raised us up with (synēgeiren)* and *seated us with (synekathisen)* him in the heavenly places in *Christ* Jesus, so that in the ages to come he might show the *extravagant (hyperballon)* richness *(ploutos)* of his *grace (charitos),* in kindness *(chrēstotēti)* toward us in *Christ* Jesus.[2]

2. Eph 2:4–7 auth. var.; cf. *kindness* in 1 Cor 13:4.

Cosmic Church, Love, and Mystery in Ephesians

According to Ephesians, believers have potential access to all of heaven's goodness and spiritual blessings while still living on earth. Then it describes God's *love* with extraordinary emphasis on the riches of God's grace and kindness:

> so that in the ages he might show forth the *extravagant (hyperballon) richness (ploutos)* of his *grace (charitos),* in *kindness (chrēstotēti)* toward us in *Christ* Jesus.[3]

As Ephesians gives further description of the church (*ekklēsia*), which is *Christ's bodily presence on earth,* the primary concern is not the status of believers *in the heavens* but with the status of gentiles, whom Paul insists are *fully* members of Christ's church *on the earth*. Ephesians describes the situation like this:

> So then, remember that at one time you gentiles by birth, called 'foreskin' by those who are called 'circumcision'—a physical circumcision made in the flesh by human hands—remember that you were at that time without *Christ,* being aliens from the commonwealth of Israel, and strangers to the covenants of promise, having no hope and without God in the world. But now in *Christ* Jesus you who once were far off have been brought near by the blood of *Christ*. For he is our *peace (eirēnē);* in his flesh he has made both groups into one and has broken down the dividing wall, that is, the hostility between us.[4]

Here we see Ephesians expanding a previous statement in Colossians which asserts:

> through him [the Son of God's love] God was pleased to reconcile to himself all things *(ta panta),* whether on earth or in heaven, by making peace *(eirēnopoiēsas)* through the blood of his cross.[5]

Ephesians applies the *blood of Christ* and *peace* in Colossians to the church (*ekklēsia*) in which circumcised Jews and uncircumcised gentiles face the challenge of living together in peace. *Christ's* church (the *body* of Christ on earth) does not have hostility within it. There is no *dividing wall* between Jews and gentiles in it. Ephesians then continues with a description of *the new humanity* that has been created by Christ's church:

---

3. Eph 2:6–7 auth. var.
4. Eph 2:11–14 auth. var.
5. Col 1:19–20.

> He (*Christ*) has made ineffectual the law with its commandments and ordinances, that he might create in himself one new humanity in place of the two, thus making *peace* (*eirēnēn*), and might reconcile both to God in one body through the cross, thus putting to death that hostility through it. So he came and preached the gospel (*euēngelisato*) of *peace* (*eirēnēn*) to you who were far off and *peace* (*eirēnēn*) to those who were near, for through him both of us have access in one Spirit to the Father.[6]

The gospel is not simply good news but the gospel of *shalōm*, peace and well-being. With this statement Ephesians includes gentiles in Jewish *shalōm*, transforming the estrangement and alienation of gentiles into *citizenship* in Christ's church:

> So then, you are no longer strangers and aliens, but you are fellow citizens (*sympolitai*) with the saints and also members of the household (*oikeioi*) of God, built upon the foundation of the apostles and prophets, with *Christ* Jesus himself as the cornerstone; in him the whole house (*oikodomē*) is joined together and grows into a holy temple (*naon*) in the Lord; in whom you also are *built together* (*synoikodomeisthe*) spiritually into a housing-place (*katoikētērion*) for God.[7]

Here we see both the *bodiliness* and *earthiness* of the church. The church is not only *in the heavenly places*. It is also on earth, where believing Jews and gentiles live together peacefully. Later in Ephesians this is restated in relation to *love*:

> speaking the truth in *love* (*agapēi*), we must grow up in every way into him who is the head, into *Christ*, from whom the whole body, joined and knitted together by every ligament with which it is equipped, as each part according to its *cosmic energy* (*energeian*) promotes the body's growth in *building itself up* (*oikodomēn heautou*) in *love* (*agapēi*).[8]

After the focus on making Jews and gentiles into *one humanity* in the second chapter and summarizing this in the fourth chapter, Ephesians focuses on *love* in Christ's church that reaches a highpoint when it discusses the relation of husbands to wives. So let us end this chapter with a discussion of *the mystery of Christ's love of the church* in relation to husbands and wives.

6. Eph 2:15–18 auth. var.
7. Eph 2:19–22 auth. var.
8. Eph 4:15–16 auth. var.

COSMIC CHURCH, LOVE, AND MYSTERY IN EPHESIANS

CHRIST'S *LOVE* BATHES THE CHURCH TO MAKE HER HOLY

It is remarkable that the most concentrated repetition of *agapē* in Ephesians occurs toward the end when it describes *Christ's love for the church* where hearers expect total focus on the relation of husbands to wives. Ephesians creates a long description of *Christ's love for the church* by expanding a simple two-part statement about husbands and wives in Colossians:

> Husbands, *love* (*agapāte*) your wives
> and do not be embittered (*pikrainesthe*) toward them.[9]

Ephesians expands the first part of the Colossians statement into a description of *Christ's love for the church* interwoven with *how a husband should love his wife*. The initial expansion is a long sentence containing amazingly vivid description of tenderly bathing one's loved one:

> Husbands, *love* (*agapāte*) your wives
> just as Christ *loved* (*ēgapēsen*) the *church* (*ekklēsian*)
> and *gave himself up* (*paredōken*) for her,
> in order to make her holy by cleansing her with the washing of water by the word,
> so as to present the *church* (*ekklēsian*) to *himself* (*heautōi*) in splendor (*endoxon*),
> without a spot or wrinkle or anything of the kind,
> so that she may be holy and without blemish.[10]

Here instead of *personifying love*, as Paul does in 1 Corinthians 13, Ephesians *personifies* the *church* (*ekklēsia*). The church is personified as *Christ's wife*. *Christ loved* the church and *handed himself over* (to be crucified) for the church, so he could *make the church holy* (*hagiasēi*) by cleansing her with the washing of water by the word. The imagery here must come from baptism. In baptism, *Christ bathes the church* to make her holy by cleansing her. *Christ's* purpose is *to present the church to himself in splendor* (*endoxon*). In other words, Christ makes *the church sparkling clean for himself!* We notice immediately how the church *builds itself up* (*oikodomēn heautou*) in *love* (*agapēi*). In the discussion of *Christ's bathing of the church*, Christ makes her beautiful, clean, and holy *for himself*. This action *for himself* is an extension of the statement in Colossians that "through *Christ* God was

---

9. Col 3:19; trans. Jeal, *Exploring Colossians*, 241.
10. Eph 5:25–27.

pleased to reconcile *to himself* all things."[11] In Ephesians, this reconciliation *through Christ* not only *brings peace* but it creates holiness as *Christ through love* tenderly bathes the church to make her sparkling clean. When *Christ's* action is complete, the church is *without a spot or wrinkle or anything of the kind.* The remarkable picture here, where the church is thoroughly *washed and ironed* for *Christ* is a reconfiguration of Solomon's desire for Wisdom as his bride, which we discussed in chapter 4:

> I loved (*ephilēsa*) her [Wisdom] and sought her from my youth; I desired to take her for my bride and became enamored of her beauty. She glorifies (*doxazei*) her noble birth by living with God, and the Lord of all loves (*ēgapēsen*) her.[12]

Solomon's desire for Wisdom as his bride with all her *glorious splendor* has been reconfigured into Christ's *love* for the Church as he bathes her in cleansing water to take her *to himself* in *splendor*.

If we wonder where Ephesians has gotten the imagery of cleansing with water, the answer lies deep within priestly configuration of water purification within Judaism. We see this imagery vividly in the Dead Sea Qumran writings. The Manual of Discipline (1QS) for the Qumran community blends wisdom with water purification in relation to truth in the following way:

> In the *mysteries* of His understanding, and in His glorious *wisdom*, God has ordained an end for injustice, and at the time of the visitation He will destroy it forever. Then *truth*, which has wallowed in the ways of wickedness during the dominion of injustice until the appointed time of judgement, shall arise in the world for ever. God will then *purify* every human deed with His *truth*; he will refine for Himself the human frame by rooting out all spirit of injustice from the bounds of his flesh. He will *cleanse* him of all wicked deeds with the spirit of *holiness*; like *purifying waters* He will shed upon him the spirit of *truth* (to cleanse him) of all abomination and injustice. And he shall be plunged into the spirit of *purification*, that he may instruct the upright in the *knowledge* of the Most High and teach the *wisdom* of the sons of heaven to those of perfect behavior.[13]

---

11. Col 1:20.
12. Wis 8:2–3.
13. 1QS 4:18–23; Vermes, *The Complete Dead Sea Scrolls in English*, 103.

Cosmic Church, Love, and Mystery in Ephesians

Ephesians configures purifying bathing imagery into marriage imagery in the discussion of husbands, wives, *Christ*, and the church that comes after this:

> In the same way, husbands should *love (agapān) their own (heautōn)* wives
> as *(hōs)* they do *their own (heautōn)* bodies.
> He who *loves (agapōn) his own (heautou)* wife
> *loves (agapāi) himself (heauton)*.
> For no one ever hates *his own (heautou)* flesh *(sarka)*,
> but he nourishes and tenderly cares for it,
> *just as Christ does for the church,*
> *because we are members of his (autou) body.*
> "For this reason a man will leave his father and mother and be joined to his wife,
> and the two will become one flesh *(sarka)*."
> *This is a great mystery,*
> *and I am speaking about Christ and the church.*[14]

This discussion of husbands and wives, which Ephesians applies to *Christ* and the church, is a revision of *loving one's neighbor as oneself (hōs heautou)*. Ephesians says husbands should love *their own (heautou)* wives as *(hōs)* they do *their own bodies*. Ephesians then closes with:

> Each of you, however, should love his wife *as himself (hōs heautou)*,
> and a wife should respect *(phobētai)* her husband.[15]

This is a revision and expansion of the second part of the statement in Colossians:

> and do not be embittered *(pikrainesthe)* toward them.[16]

In Ephesians, *loving one's neighbor as oneself* has become both *husbands loving their wives as themselves* and *Christ's loving the church as himself*. When husbands act *lovingly* toward their wives, they are *embodying* the *truth* of *Christ's self* both on earth and in heaven. *Christ* is God's *love* enacted on earth as it is in heaven.

---

14. Eph 5:28–32 auth. var.
15. Eph 5:33.
16. Col 3:18.

CONCLUSION

As we conclude this chapter it will be good to reflect back on our journey with Paul's letters. We started in 1 Corinthians with *wisdom* becoming *personified love*. There we observed how Paul *fills* love with actions that *build up* the church. *Love*, therefore, does not cause quarrels, disputes, and disagreements but is patient and kind. Colossians takes Paul's concept of *love* much further. Colossians *fills* love with the *richness* of God's *wisdom* and *truth*, which extends far beyond avoiding quarrels into *being made alive with Christ* through the re-creating *cosmic energy (energeia)* that is in both God and *Christ*. Ephesians, building on Colossians, presents Paul's role in bringing *God's love* into the world in the following way:

> Of this gospel I have become a servant according to the gift of God's grace that was given me by the working of his power. Although I am the very least of all the saints, this grace was given to me to bring to the gentiles the news of the boundless riches of *Christ* and *to make everyone see what is the plan of the mystery hidden for ages in God, who created all things*, so that through the church *the wisdom of God* in its rich variety might now be made known to the rulers and authorities in the heavenly places.[17]

For Ephesians, God's love becomes *the plan of the mystery hidden for ages in God who created all things*. Thus, Paul's prayer for believers in Ephesians is as follows:

> I pray that you may have the power to comprehend, with all the saints, what is the breadth and length and height and depth and to *know the love of Christ* that surpasses knowledge, so that you may be *filled* with all the *fullness* of God.[18]

In the end, then, God's love through Christ is a *mystery*. This takes us back to 1 Corinthians where Paul described Christ as God's wisdom, *mysterious and hidden* until *Christ* comes. Ephesians moves beyond this by revising *loving one's neighbor as oneself* into *Christ loving the church as himself* and a husband *loving his wife as himself*. Ephesians claims that:

> He who *loves* his own wife *loves himself*.[19]

---

17. Eph 3:7–10.
18. Eph 3:18–19.
19. Eph 5:28.

Cosmic Church, Love, and Mystery in Ephesians

The mystery here is God's *wisdom*, secret and hidden, in *Christ's love for the church*. This *mystery* is as great as the mystery of a man and his wife becoming *one flesh*. Ephesians ends with:

> *Peace* (*eirēnē*) be to the brothers and sisters and *love* (*agapē*) with faith, from God the Father and the Lord Jesus *Christ*. *Grace* (*charis*) be with all who have an undying *love* (*agapōntōn*) for our Lord Jesus *Christ*.[20]

By the end of Ephesians, then, *love of God* has been transformed into *love of Christ*. We started on our journey in Mark with the Jewish Shema, which emphasizes *loving God with one's whole heart, soul, mind, and strength*. Here in this chapter on Ephesians we have come to the Christian revision of the Shema into *loving Christ with undying love*. In 1 Corinthians 13, Paul spoke of *love* as *never failing*. Ephesians ends with a benediction that prays for *love of Christ* that *never dies*. May it be so for all who start the journey of *reciprocal love* of God through Christ.

QUESTIONS FOR DISCUSSION

1. Do you envision the church you attend as extending into *heavenly places* where Christ is seated at the right hand of God?
2. Do you experience *God's love* filled with *divine wisdom* in Christ's church?
3. Do you see God's love breaking down *a dividing wall* in the church you attend?
4. Can you picture God's love *bathing you* with tender *loving* care in the church you attend?

---

20. Eph 6:23–24.

8

God Is Love in 1 John

God is love,
and those who abide in love abide in God,
and God abides in them.[1]

IN PREVIOUS CHAPTERS WE have seen how Jesus became a cosmic being in early Christianity. In the gospel of John, we saw how Jesus became the only-begotten Son of the Father through a *cosmic story* in which the Son brings eternal life into the world. The Son does this through his agency as *logos* Word who lays down his living being and takes it up again in obedience to the Father's command. The Son's obedience to God's commands introduces a *chain of love, commandment,* and *abiding*. This *chain* presents *life* flowing from the Father through the Son to believers who are commanded to love one another as the Son loves them. In Colossians we saw how the *cosmic story* of the Son is transformed into a *cosmic picture* in which the Son reconciles all things to himself, making peace through the blood of his cross, whether things on the earth or things in the heavens.[2] In Colossians *love* is filled with wisdom, understanding, and knowledge that reshapes Jewish *shalōm* into *fullness* that brings peace, well-being, and reconciliation to all things throughout the cosmos. In Ephesians we saw how the *cosmic picture* in Colossians is reshaped in terms of God's love bringing forth a new

1. 1 John 4:16.
2. Col 1:18–20.

humanity where Jews and gentiles live together in unity in Christ's Church. This church is nurtured, cared for, and *bathed* by Christ so it becomes a place of renewal, refreshment, and fulfillment for all believers.

GOD IS LOVE IN 1 JOHN

As we turn to the first epistle of John, we see a transformation of the *cosmic story* in the gospel of John of the love of God's only-begotten Son into a discussion that focuses on God's love. As 1 John does this, there are almost three times as many occurrences of the noun *agapē* in 1 John (18) as in the gospel of John (7).[3] For 1 John the issue is if *God's love* is *in* a believer. If God's love is in a believer, then this believer loves others (a *verbal* emphasis). If a person does *not* love (verbal) a brother or sister, then God's love is *not* in them. In the gospel of John, in contrast, there is an emphasis that "the Father loves (verbal) the Son" and the Son "loves (verbal) both the Father and his own." If people love (verbal) the Son, then *the Son's love* is in them, they love one another, and the Father also loves them. Thus, the gospel of John focuses on the Father and the Son, and the special focus is on the Son and his love. This is regularly described as a *christological* emphasis, namely an emphasis on Jesus as God's messiah (*christos*) who loves both the Father and *his own*. The focus on *God's love* in 1 John, in contrast, means that 1 John is *theological*—it emphasizes the nature of God as *loving*. This theological focus reaches its highest point in the author's assertion twice that God *is* love. The circular nature of *God's love* is central in 1 John. First, the author emphasizes the action of love in a negative statement: "Whoever does *not love* (verbal) does not know God, for *God is love*."[4] If a person does not *love* (others, the Son, and God), then this person does *not know* God nor have God's love *in* them. In 1 John love *circulates* from God through believers back to God in the form of *knowing* God. Later in 1 John the author describes the nature of love through the process of *abiding*: "God *is love*, and those who abide in *love* abide in *God*, and God abides *in* them."[5] God's love, then, is a *presence* that is *active*. Those who *enact* love have *love in them*, and those in whom love is present enact love in *the way they believe and live*.

---

3. John 5:42; 13:25; 15:9–10, 13; 17:26; 1 John 2:5, 15; 3:1, 16–17; 4:7–10, 12, 16–18; 5:3.
4. 1 John 4:8.
5. 1 John 4:16.

Finding Love

First John sets its assertions in motion with a summary of the prologue to the Gospel of John that *announces* what happened in the *cosmic story* about the Word. The summary emphasizes "what we have heard, what we have seen with our eyes, what we have looked at and touched with our hands, concerning the word of life."[6] Then it continues with, "This life was manifested (made *present* in the world), and we have seen it and testify to it, and declare to you the eternal life that was with the Father and was manifested (made *present*) to us."[7] Then it announces that "what we have seen and heard we also declare to you so that you also may have *fellowship* (*koinōnia*) with us, and truly our *fellowship* (*koinōnia*) is with the Father and with his Son Jesus Christ. We are writing these things so that our joy may be complete."[8] After the summary focuses on the *life* that was *made present* in the Word that they have *heard, seen,* and *touched* it asserts that this *life* has made clear that *God is light*: "This is the message (*angelia*) we have heard from him and announce (*anangellomen*) to you, that *God is light* and in him is no darkness at all."[9] Why is the emphasis on God as *light*? The answer lies in the way this life *vividly shows* us how to *walk in the way of God's love*. This approach lies first and foremost in the gospel of John. But the answer also lies elsewhere in early Christian belief, and we will especially notice aspects of it in the gospel of Matthew.

WALKING IN THE LIGHT OF GOD'S LOVE

If we look carefully back at the prologue to John we can notice that it asserts: "What has come into being in him (the Word) was life, and the life was the light of all people. The Light shines in the darkness, and the darkness did not overtake it."[10] First John reshapes these words in the gospel John into statements about *fellowship* grounded in theological belief in God as light:

> This is the message we have heard from him and proclaim to you, that *God is light* and in him there is no darkness at all. If we say that we have *fellowship* with him while we are walking in darkness, we lie and do not do what is true; but *if we walk in the light* as he

---

6. 1 John 1:1.
7. 1 John 1:2 auth. var.
8. 1 John 1:3–4.
9. 1 John 1:5 auth. var.
10. John 1:3–5.

> *himself is in the light*, we have *fellowship* with one another, and the blood of Jesus his Son cleanses us from all sin.[11]

The focus on *believers walking in God's light* is the rewording in 1 John of the christological assertion in the gospel of John that "The true light, which enlightens everyone, was coming into the world (namely, the Word)...to all who received him, who believed in his name, he gave power to become *children of God*."[12] Children of God have fellowship with God and with Jesus, and they also have fellowship with other believers. This fellowship is enabled through the blood of Jesus which cleanses all from sin. In other words, rather than emphasizing that the blood of the cross brings *reconciliation* and *peace*, as asserted in Colossians, in 1 John the emphasis is God's removal of *sin* through the Word of Life, which is a rewording of the pronouncement by John the Baptist in the gospel of John that Jesus is "the Lamb of God who takes away the sin of the world."[13] This means that the Word's *christological enactment* of love in the world was the means by which the *theological nature* of God as love brought removal of sin into the world.

In the midst of this, it is fascinating how the emphasis on light in 1 John is related to assertions in the gospel of Matthew. First, there is an assertion in Matthew that:

> the people who sat in darkness have seen a great *light*, and for those who sat in the region and shadow of death *light* has dawned.[14]

Then later in Matthew there is an assertion by Jesus that:

> *You* are the *light* of the world. A city built on a hill cannot be hid. People do not light a lamp and put it under the bushel basket; rather, they put it on the lampstand, and it gives *light* to all in the house. *In the same way*, let *your light* shine before others, so that they may see your good works and give glory to your Father in heaven.[15]

And further on in Matthew Jesus emphasizes the possibility of *darkness* in one's body rather than *light*:

---

11. 1 John 1:5–7.
12. John 1:9, 12.
13. John 1:29.
14. Matt 4:16.
15. Matt 5:14–16.

> The eye is the lamp of the body. So if your eye is healthy, your whole body will be full of *light*, but if your eye is unhealthy, your whole body will be full of *darkness*. If, then, the *light in you* is *darkness*, how great is the *darkness*![16]

A sharp distinction between *light* and *darkness* is in both the gospel of Matthew and the gospel of John, but in 1 John and Matthew there is an emphasis on light or darkness *in believers* rather than *in the world*. In the gospel of John, the emphasis is on darkness *in the world* rather than *in the believer*. In Matthew the emphasis is on the *eye* (what believers have *seen*) as the agent of *light* in the body.

After 1 John introduces the topic of *walking in the light*, there is a discussion of *love* versus *hate*:

> Whoever says, "*I am in the light*," while *hating* a brother or sister, is still in the *darkness*. Whoever *loves* a brother or sister abides in the *light*, and in such a person there is no cause for stumbling. But whoever *hates* a brother or sister is in the *darkness*, *walks* in the *darkness*, and does not know the way to go, because the *darkness* has brought on blindness.[17]

The discussion of *hate* in relation to *love* represents yet another relationship to Matthew, where Jesus says:

> You have heard that it was said, "You shall *love* your neighbor and *hate* your enemy." But I say to you: *Love* your enemies and pray for those who persecute you, so that you may be *children of your Father in heaven*.[18]

While in Matthew Jesus discusses love and hate in relation to one's *neighbor* and *enemy,* 1 John focuses on *brothers* and *sisters*. In 1 John, therefore, there is an implication that believers live in a *family* relationship as *children* of God in a manner related to Jesus' relation to God as *his only-begotten Son*. Deeply embedded in this *family* relationship is *obedience to the Father*. First John emphasizes that "the Son obeyed the commandment of the Father," and this activity of *obedience* carries down through the Son to "those who love God," who "*must* love their brothers and sisters also."[19] 1 John puts it this way:

16. Matt 6:22–23.
17. 1 John 2:9–11.
18. Matt 5:43–45.
19. 1 John 4:21.

> Everyone who believes that Jesus is the Christ has been born of God, and everyone who loves the parent loves the child. By this we know that we love *the children of God*, when we love God and obey his commandments.[20]

Parents love their children and God the Father loves both his only-begotten Son and all humans as his children on earth. All who *believe* that Jesus is the Messiah are *born* of God and are *children of God*. When believers *love God*, they also *love* the children of God. This is the *obedience* Jesus has modeled for all humans and which all humans who *believe* in God and his only Son also perform. This is the *new* commandment and *new* obedience (in the gospel of John) that is the *old* commandment and obedience embedded in the *love of God* for the world (in 1 John). As it says in 1 John:

> Beloved, I am writing you *no new commandment* but an *old* commandment that you have had from the beginning; the *old* commandment is the word that you have heard. Yet I am writing you a *new* commandment that is true in him and in you, because the darkness is passing away and the true light is already shining.[21]

It is fascinating how this discussion of the *new* and the *old* is related to Jesus' statement in Matthew:

> Every scribe who has become a disciple in the kingdom of heaven is like the master of a household who brings out of his treasure *what is new* and *what is old*.[22]

In Matthew, what is new is the *new Torah* that Jesus brings out of *old Torah* with the aid of the Prophets. What is new in 1 John is the *new commandment*: love one another with God's love that is in you. This new commandment is a transformation of the *old commandment,* "Love one another as I have loved you." This *old* commandment becomes *new* when one *sees* and *knows* that *love* is God's love. For 1 John, love is both *in God* and *is God*, because *God is love*. The *love* in humans, therefore, is *God's love*. This *love* comes *from God* and is *present* in humans when humans love one another and love God.

---

20. 1 John 5:1–2.
21. 1 John 2:7–8.
22. Matt 13:52.

Finding Love

A THEOLOGY OF LOVE

The special theology of *love* in 1 John becomes a five-step argument in 1 John 4:7–12.[23] The argument progresses from the *origin* of love to the *practice* of love in the following manner:[24]

1. Origin of Love (4:7–10)
2. Answer of Love (4:11–12)
3. Experience of Love (4:13–16)
4. Future of Love (4:17–18)
5. Practice of Love (4:19–21)

If we work carefully through this outline, we will be able to enter deeply, fully, and profoundly into the theology of *love* in 1 John.

IN THE BEGINNING WAS GOD'S LOVE

1. Origin of Love: 4:7–10:

> Beloved, let us *love* one another, because *love* is from God; everyone who *loves* is born of God and *knows* God. Whoever does *not love* does *not know* God, for God is *love*. God's love *was* manifested among us in this way: God sent his only Son into the world so that we might live through him. In this is *love, not that we loved God* but that *he loved us* and sent his Son to be the atoning sacrifice for our sins.

Love originates with God. *Love abides* as the innermost nature of God within *life* that comes into our fleshly being from God. First John, therefore, embeds *love* within both *life* and *eternal life* as they are presented in the gospel of John. Within both *life* and *eternal life* is *God's love*. *We* are the product of God's love, which comes through life into our fleshly being. As *we* live and move and have our being, therefore, we truly *live within God* with *God's innermost nature* within us if we *love* those with whom we live. This mode

---

23. Oda Wischmeyer, *Love as Agape: The Early Christian Concept and Modern Discourse* (Waco: Baylor University Press, 2021) 120–29, following Hans-Josef Klauck, *Der erste Johannesbrief* (Evangelisch-Katholischer Kommentar zum Neuen Testament 23; Neukirchen-Vluyn: Neukirchener, 1991) 245–73.

24. Wischmeyer, *Love as Agape*, 125.

God Is Love in 1 John

of *living together in love* reaches its highest point in removal of sin through the *love of God's Son* and in the *fullness* of *fellowship* with *brothers and sisters* which is *at the same time* fellowship with God the Father and his Son:

> We declare to you the everlasting life that was with the Father and was manifested to us—what we have seen and heard we also declare to you so that you also may have *fellowship* with us, and truly our *fellowship is with the Father and with his Son Jesus Christ*. We are writing these things so that our joy may be *filled* (*peplērōmenē*).[25]

At this point, *historical sequence* seems to disappear in *fullness*. It is not the case that fellowship *begins* with brothers and sisters and then *becomes* fellowship with God and Jesus Christ. Rather, fellowship with other people who believe *is at the same time* fellowship with God the Father and with his Son Jesus Christ. This fellowship becomes a relationship of *fullness*, *because* it is fellowship *both* with other humans *and* with God and his Son Jesus. Fullness, therefore, is not an *event* in time. It is a *relationship* in which fellowship with other humans is *at the same time* a relationship with God and his Son.

LOVING ONE ANOTHER AS GOD LOVES US

2. Answer of Love: 4:11–12:

> Beloved, since God loved us so much, we also ought to love one another. No one has ever seen God; if we love one another, God abides in us, and his love is *perfected* in us.

At this point the argument in 1 John moves to an *inner* form of obligation: "We also *ought* to love one another." "Astonishingly, it is not love for *God* but now specifically love for *brothers* and *sisters* that connects people to God, for the *direct vision of God* and thus a *direct love relationship* is not *possible*."[26] At it says in the gospel of John, "No one has ever seen God." It is only through seeing *the Son* that we see God. This *seeing* enables the enactment of the *love-commandment-abiding chain* the gospel of John presents in its storyline. First John expands this *chain of love* into a *fellowship-chain* that emphasizes *interactive* brotherly and sisterly love that is at the same

---

25. 1 John 1:2–4 auth. var.
26. Wischmeyer, *Love as Agape*, 126.

time *interactive fellowship* with God and with Jesus Christ. Since this *fellowship* is like the Son's relation to the Father, the obedience of the Son brings removal of sin to believers. This means that *love* on earth has an *inner-interactive* dimension with brothers and sisters, with the Son, and with God. The *inner* nature of this *fellowship* is its *interactivity* among brothers and sisters which is *at same time* interactivity with God and God's Son Jesus Christ. In the language of 1 John, this *fellowship* is *perfected love*. This *fellowship* emerges out of *obedience* to the commandment to "love bothers and sisters" which, perhaps without knowing it (!), fulfills the commandment in Matthew to "Be *perfect* as your heavenly Father is *perfect*."[27]

KNOWING THAT WE ABIDE IN GOD'S LOVE

3. Experience of Love: 4:13–16:

> By this we *know* that we *abide* in him and he in us, because he has given us of his Spirit. 14 And we have seen and do testify that the Father has sent his Son as the Savior of the world. 15 God *abides* in those who confess that Jesus is the Son of God, and they *abide* in God. 16 So *we have known and believe the love* that God has for us. God is love, and those who abide in *love* abide in *God*, and God abides in them.

What believers *know* in 1 John is that they abide in God and God abides in them. They also know that God has given them his Spirit. The initial statement about the origin of *love* in God made both a positive and a negative statement about *knowing*: "Everyone who *loves* . . . knows God; whoever does *not love* does *not know* God, for God is love."[28] Believers *know* the *abiding* chain. They experience God more fully by *knowing* their abiding in God.

In 1 John, the emphasis is on "knowing" (*ginōskein*) Jesus Christ and keeping his commandments.[29] The major commandment is to "believe in the name of his Son Jesus Christ and love one another, just as he has commanded us."[30] The foundation of this is believing "the love that God has for us." This means a belief that "God is love, and those who abide in love abide

---

27. Matt 5:48.
28. 1 John 4:7–8.
29. 1 John 2:3.
30. 1 John 3:23; cf. 5:13.

in God, and God abides in them."³¹ All of this means believing that Jesus is the Son of God, which means that Jesus is the Messiah born of God.³²

LIVING IN GOD'S PERFECTED LOVE

4. Future of Love: 4:17–18:

> Love has been *perfected* among us in this: that we may have boldness on the day of judgement, because as he is, so are we in this world. 18 There is no fear in love, but *perfect love* casts out fear; for fear has to do with punishment, and whoever fears has not reached *perfection* in love.

First John introduces the concept of *perfection* when it moves beyond *love* versus *hate* into *commandment* and *obedience* in 1 John 2:5–6:

> whoever *obeys* his word, truly in this person the love of God has reached *perfection*. By this we may be sure that we are in him: 6 whoever says, "I abide in him," ought to walk just as he walked.

Then 1 John 4:12 explains this *perfection* in this manner:

> No one has ever seen God; if we love one another, God lives in us, and *his love is perfected in us*.

Rather than simply asserting "Be *perfect* as your heavenly Father is *perfect*," as we see in the gospel of Matthew,³³ 1 John builds on the *love-commandment-abiding chain* in the gospel of John. The emphasis on "no one has ever seen God" means that no one except the Son has the ability to "imitate" *God's perfection*. But *imitating* the *obedience* of God's Son creates *perfection of love* in believers, since God's love *abides* in those who *believe*.

Through a theology of *perfected love*, 1 John completely changes an understanding of fear. According to Wisdom tradition, "Fear (*phobos*) of God is the beginning of wisdom (*sophia*)."³⁴ In 1 John, "There is *no fear* in love, but *perfect love drives out fear*, for fear reckons with punishment, but the one who fears has not come to perfection in love."³⁵

31. 1 John 4:16.
32. 1 John 5:1; cf. 5:5, 10.
33. Matt 5:48.
34. Prov 1:7.
35. 1 John 4:18.

Finding Love

OBEYING GOD'S COMMANDMENT TO LOVE ONE ANOTHER

5. Practice of Love: 4:19–21:

> We love because he first loved us. 20 Those who say, "I love God," and hate their brothers or sisters, are liars; for those who do not love a brother or sister whom they have seen, cannot love God whom they have not seen. 21 The *commandment* we have from him is this: those who love God must love their brothers and sisters also.

When both the gospel of John and 1 John introduce the topic of *love,* "the starting point . . . lies in and with God."[36] Starting with *God's love for the world* reverses the direction of love in the Jewish Shema, where humans hear the call "to *love* the Lord your God with all your heart, soul, and mind." Rather than starting with a commandment for humans to *love God*, both the gospel of John and 1 John emphasize that God loves the world and loves all humans in it.

Within time, God *first* loved us. But now, according to 1 John, *time* is embedded so deeply in *relationship* that *believing activity* is virtually *timeless.* This calls to mind the response of the *righteous* in Matthew 25 when they say, "*When* did we see you thirsty and give you drink, etc."[37] The righteous did not experience their actions as *events* but simply as *relationships.* They were so deeply invested in *relationships* of *love* that they were not conscious of these actions as *things they did in time* but simply as *natural bodily relationships* that they had with other humans in need. In 1 John these *natural relationships* bring *fullness of joy* into daily well-being (*shalōm*). This belief energizes the *flow of life and love* from God through the Son into the believer. Similarly, in Matthew Jesus tells the rich young man, "If you wish to enter into *life,* keep the commandments."[38]

---

36. Wischmeyer, *Love as Agape*, 156.
37. Matt 25:31–46.
38. Matt 19:17.

God Is Love in 1 John

CONCLUSION

For 1 John, God is love. This means that the life in our bodies contains love deep within it. Our lives have come out of God's love. God's forming of us is a manifestation (presence) of God's love. This love is present in our ability to see, hear, taste, smell, feel, and know where parts of our body are at any time. If we know the *cosmic story* in the gospel of John, where God's love sent God's Son into the world, and *believe* this story, then we can *know* that God's love abides in us. In turn, God's love in us enables and guides us in our love for others. This love for others fulfills God's commandment to "love one another," and it introduces *fellowship* not only with other believers but also with God and his Son. This fellowship creates an environment whereby *perfected love* energizes God's removal of sin from our lives. This perfected love, of course, has been made known to us through the storyline of the gospel of John, but according to 1 John, if we *know* that God's love abides in us and we *love* one another, this love can grow in us into a mature, complete form it calls *fullness*. This fullness becomes present and remains present when we love both our brothers and sisters and God and his Son through our obedience of loving one another as God loves us. May this possibility ever be so.

QUESTIONS FOR DISCUSSION

1. What do you think about the shift of focus from *Jesus'* love for his followers to *God's* love for all in the world in 1 John? In other words, do you like a *theological* focus on love more than a *christological* focus on love? Explain.

2. While *life* and *eternal life* are emphasized repetitively in the *gospel* of John, the letter of 1 John emphasizes *love* within God and within humans. Do you like one emphasis better than the other? If so, why? If not, why not?

3. Do you think it is possible to be a Christian without emphasizing that *God is love*? If so, explain how this might be possible. If it is not possible, explain why you think it is not possible.

4. While *fellowship (koinōnia)* never occurs in the gospels of Mark, Matthew, Luke, or John, it occurs four times in 1 John. Why do you think

the concept of fellowship does not occur in any of the gospels, but it does occur in the first chapter of 1 John?

5. This chapter asserts that there is an interesting relationship between the role of *light* in the gospel of Matthew and 1 John. Do you agree that the relationship is interesting? Or do you think it is more important to call attention simply to the relation of light in the gospel of John and 1 John? Explain.

6. Were you surprised by the assertion of the author of 1 John that "I am writing you *no new commandment*, but an *old* commandment that you have had from the beginning; the *old* commandment is the word that you have heard" (1 John 2:7)? Why do you think the writer of 1 John can call the *new commandment* in the gospel of John an *old* commandment? Explain.

7. Do you think it possible for *God's love* to be in a person? Or is the love within a person always *human love*? Explain.

8. Do you think it is possible for *love* within a person to become *perfect love* that casts out *fear*? Or is this an *ideal* that can never be realized in a human being? Explain.

9. Do you think the emphasis on *commandment* conflicts with the emphasis on *God's love* in 1 John? In other words, do you think being *obedient* to a *commandment to love* is different from *living in a relationship of love* which a person does not think of as a *commandment*? Explain.

Conclusion

This is my prayer,
that your love may overflow
more and more with knowledge and full insight.[1]

WE HAVE LEARNED MANY things on our journey together in this book. Chief among them is an awareness that Christianity is the stream of Judaism that transformed Torah law into Messiah-oriented wisdom and love. During the second temple period, Judaism was transforming Torah law into wisdom, and followers of Jesus emerged during this transition in Judaism. After the destruction of Jerusalem and its temple in 70 CE, two major streams of Judaism gradually established themselves in the Mediterranean world. One stream maintained a faithfulness to Hebrew and Aramaic language, as well as a faithfulness to the inner spirit of temple Judaism. We regularly refer to this as rabbinic Judaism, and its major texts are the Tanakh, Mishnah, and the Jerusalem and Babylonian Talmuds. The other stream adopted Greek as its major language and transformed the inner spirit of the Torah and the Prophets into poetic wisdom focused on Jesus as God's Messiah and God's love. This stream produced the New Testament and writings of the Church Fathers and is regularly called Christianity.

As this Greek-speaking *Christ-believing* Judaism spread throughout the Mediterranean world and beyond, new institutional forms emerged in both streams of Judaism. Alongside rabbinic academies and synagogues, *Christ*-believing household assemblies (*ekklēsia*) and bishoprics emerged in the messianic Jewish stream, and these began to claim the attention of Roman emperors. When Constantine declared Christianity to be the

1. Phil 1:9.

religion of the Roman empire during the fourth century CE, the heritage of messianic Judaism moved into the center of the Roman empire. This mode of Judaism called Christianity moved to center stage during the final centuries of the Roman empire. Then it entered the thriving vibrancy of the Byzantine empire and participated in a trialogue among Judaism, Christianity, and Islam until the Medieval period emerged.

If you had asked me prior to writing this book what Christianity achieved during its rise to prominence, I would have said it created a new *paideia*, namely a new system of education in the Mediterranean world. Werner Jaeger popularized this idea in *Early Christianity and Greek Paideia* in 1961,[2] and there is great insight in this point of view. But when interpreting Christianity in its Jewish setting, it becomes clear that *Christ*-believers transformed the wisdom in the Wisdom books in the Greek Old Testament into messianic Jesus wisdom and love. A major influence in the background of this transformation was Greek philosophy, which emphasized the importance of disciplined thinking which led to the control of one's passions and emotions. Since, in the view of messianic *Christ*-believers, *Christ* Jesus had been crucified, buried, resurrected, and exalted into heaven, God's *wisdom* and *love* emphasized suffering and death. Through the writings of these *Christ*-believers, *wisdom* became *love-wisdom* that cares for others as it *builds up* believing communities.

So, if we were to summarize what we have learned in this book, what would we say? In the first chapter we learned that *the messianic secret* in Mark might actually refer to God's love hiding in the coming of the kingdom of God. When the Gentile soldier sees Jesus die on the cross toward the end of Mark and says, "Truly this was a son of God,"[3] he is not far from knowing the secret, but does he *know* that God *loves* Jesus? No one except Peter, James, and John hear the voice of God saying that Jesus is loved by God, but they are so filled with fear and lack of understanding that they surely do not get it. Many interpreters say the demons know who Jesus is when they call him Son of God.[4] But it seems that the demons also have no way of *knowing* that God *loves* Jesus.

Chapter two presents Jesus' reshaping of six commandments from the Torah in the beginning of the Sermon on the Mount that reaches a climax

---

2. Werner Jaeger, *Early Christianity and Greek Paideia* (Cambridge, MA: Belknap, 1961).

3. Mark 15:39 auth. trans.

4. Mark 3:12; 5:7.

CONCLUSION

in the commandment to *love your enemies*. In other words, in Matthew Jesus emphasizes *loving one's enemies* as the highpoint of his reshaping of the Torah. This *love* comes into Jesus' teaching on the wings of the Torah and the Prophets. The intensification of both the Torah and the Prophets leads to assertions about God as *perfect* and of the necessity to *be perfect* as God is *perfect*. When we searched for the special emphasis on *perfection*, we were led to the Qumran Dead Sea Community run by priestly leaders and their distinction between *children of light* and *children of darkness*. This discussion led us to a view of *perfection* in the gospel of Matthew as mature, fully-developed, complete *love* as it is expressed in *love of one's enemies*.

In Chapter three we saw that the Sermon on the Plain in Luke presents Jesus turning immediately to the topic of *loving one's enemies* after beatitudes announcing blessings on the poor and woes on those who are rich. Jesus' teaching about *loving of enemies* flows out of, "Woe to you when all speak well of you, for that is what their ancestors did to the false prophets."[5] Here we see Jesus putting his followers in the position of the prophets, who faced rejection, abuse, and sometimes even death for speaking out against injustices in Israelite society. In other words, Jesus' statements about *love* in the Sermon on the Plain are *prophetic wisdom*. Jesus calls his disciples and the readers of this gospel to challenge the rich and powerful to care for the poor and marginalized, even as the rich and powerful take action against them for doing so. Perhaps all of us feel deeply challenged by this voice from scripture. How much will we lend to the poor out of our abundance, "expecting nothing in return"?

For chapter four, we learned about the possibility of translating *agapē* love as *she* rather than *it* in 1 Corinthians 13. The reason is that Paul is reshaping Sophia wisdom into *love* that guides people in what they should do and should not do to *build up* the community. After transforming God's *wisdom* into statements of what "*Love* does . . . and *love* does not do . . .," to *build up* community, Paul *fills* God's love with the story of *Christ* as the dying-rising-exalted Messiah. The key is that God's wisdom becomes God's love *through Jesus as God's Messiah*, God's *Christ*. This is not through any *teaching by Jesus*. *Wisdom* becomes *love* through God's resurrection of Christ out of the dead. Paul moves beyond the Law by transforming the Torah and the Prophets into God's *love*, which is both *God's* and *Christ's love*.

Chapter five on the gospel of John flows out of chapter four on Paul's early letters. In John, God's wisdom becomes *logos word* who becomes flesh

---

5. Luke 6:26.

Finding Love

as Jesus Christ on earth. The time of Jesus on earth is part of *a cosmic story* in which Jesus teaches and enacts God's *love* for the world. As the story unfolds, all who hear, understand, and *do* the words Jesus teaches receive *everlasting life*. The *cosmic story* itself becomes the focus of belief. All who believe that Jesus *Christ* is *logos* who created heaven and earth, *became flesh, tented* on earth, and taught and enacted God's *love* by laying down his living being and taking it up again, receive everlasting life.

In chapter six we saw the letter to the Colossians transforming the *cosmic story* in the gospel of John into a *cosmic picture* of God's love flowing into the world through Christ as the *firstborn* of all creation and the *firstborn* from the dead. As *firstborn*, the Son is *head* of all things, including the church (*ekklēsia*). In Colossians the church is envisioned as a *cosmic body* extending from *above* the heavens and the earth down throughout all the earth. A major dimension of this church is the *peace energy* that *houses* in it. This *peace energy* was active in the exaltation of *Christ above* after his crucifixion and reconciled all things to one another, bringing *peace* into the world. Those who *believe* enter into the *fullness* of God's church, where God's love is energized through the mystery of God's *love* through his Son Jesus Christ. Through God's love, believers are made alive in Christ and transferred into the *kingdom* of the Son of God's love and light through Christ's death and resurrection. This love promises to unite believers in love and fill them with full knowledge of God's mystery, which is Christ himself, in whom are hidden all the treasures of wisdom and knowledge.

In chapter seven we saw how the letter to the Ephesians presents God's love as creating a new humanity in Christ's church. In this church, which has broken down the walls of division, Jews and gentiles live together in peace and love for one another. In addition, through the mystery of Christ's love of the church, love becomes *holiness* that purifies the spirit of believers and cleanses them from their sins. Thus, God's love is fulfilled in Christ's love for the church, which fills believers with wisdom that becomes personified love as the richness of God's wisdom and truth enlivens their activity of building up the church. In Ephesians, this love is the plan of the mystery hidden for ages in God who created all things. Through this mystery love of God as it is expressed in the Jewish Shema is transformed not only into loving God but also into loving Christ with undying love. The final prayer in Ephesians is that this love of Christ may never die.

In chapter eight we saw how in the letter of 1 John love of God, love of Christ, and love of one another moves the author to assert that *God is love*.

Conclusion

Love comes from God as *light* in whom believers may walk by loving their brothers and sisters. This love activates fellowship not only among brothers and sisters but also with God and his Son Jesus Christ. Through this fellowship, the love within believers becomes *God's love* which is *perfected* through obedience to the new commandment to love one another. In 1 John, the love in believers, therefore, becomes more that Christ's love fulfilled in loving one another. The love in believers is actually *God's love* that is present and active through fellowship with other believers at the same time as it is present and active with God and his Son Jesus Christ. This love becomes more than *special events within time*. Rather, this love becomes an *abiding relationship with others* that is *at the same time* an abiding relationship with God and his Son.

A special aspect of this journey through the Bible has been the presence of influence from the Greek Old Testament. The inclusion of the Wisdom of Solomon and Sirach in our discussion brought into Judaism supplemental retellings of the story of Wisdom that expand her functions beyond Proverbs in the Hebrew Bible. After God created Wisdom and she participated in God's creation of the heavens and the earth, she journeyed through the heavens before she went to earth. After she went to earth, she *tented* with Israel until Solomon built the temple in Jerusalem. Then she *housed* herself in the temple, but she also dwelt within Solomon to guide him in discerning the inner nature of righteousness. The stream of Judaism we call Christianity expanded on this transformation of the Torah and the Prophets into God's wisdom and love.

And now there is one more item of unfinished business. I promised in the Introduction to ponder why *agapē love* is absent in the Acts of the Apostles except for one reference in Acts 15:25 to "beloved Barnabas and Paul." Why did the author of Acts, whom most think was the author of the gospel of Luke, not put *agapē love* on the lips of Paul in his speeches? Surely this means that the author did not know the letters of Paul. Otherwise, *love* surely would have occurred at least once in a speech of Paul! This must mean that Paul's conversational language daily in the context of tentmaking, and even public speechmaking of Paul that the author of Acts heard, did not use the words and conceptuality of *agapē love* frequently enough that they jumped out as distinctive language of Paul. Perhaps, then, Paul formulated *agapē love* terminology and conceptuality specifically while dictating his letters to scribes, who wrote them down. In other words, in the immediacy, inspiration, and creativity of oral composition in the face-to-face process of dictating the letters, Paul's affection for his companions and the group effort of writing the letters energized his *love* for the people he knew in the communities to which he wrote. In this context, *love* came to expression in his speech. We are fortunate that we have enough of Paul's letters that we can trace some of the emergence of his terminology and conceptuality about *love* in them.

The goal for our journey together has been to find out how *agapē love* became a central topic in early Christianity. When we got to the gospel of John, we began to see the *fullness* of God within *agapē love*. In the *cosmic story* of God's *love* in the gospel of John, God's *love* continually flows from above through the heavens to earth. The key for believers, then, is to *know* and *believe* that Jesus abides in God, God abides in Jesus, and those who abide in God abide in God's love and God's love abides in them. This is stated directly in 1 John 4:15–16:

> God abides in those who confess that Jesus is the Son of God, and they abide in God. So we have known and believe the love that God has for us. God is love, and those who abide in love abide in God, and God abides in them.[6]

With this understanding of the *centrality* of *agapē love* in Christian belief, we are equipped to begin to write a comprehensive *theology* of *agapē love* for the Christian community, and possibly for the world. But this is too big a project to tackle in this book. In truth, we have only taken a peek into *God's love*. But it is a significant peek enabled through the whims of human history. What we see at the end of this journey is that we are only at the beginning of what it could mean for our lives and for the world in which we live if the rich content and wide-reaching horizons of this *love* could live within all people in our world, and we ourselves could continually live within this *love*.

---

6. 1 John 4:15–16.

Conclusion

QUESTIONS FOR DISCUSSION

1. Do you agree that "Christianity is the stream of Judaism that transformed Torah law into Messiah-oriented wisdom and love"? If yes, why do you agree? If you do not agree, why not?

2. When Christianity moved into the center of the Roman empire, do you think this was an important achievement for Judaism as well as Christianity? Or do you think this was an achievement for Christianity that was a detriment or hindrance for Judaism? Explain.

3. Do you like the emphasis on Christian love as love *wisdom*? Or do you think *love* in Christianity should not be described as a type of wisdom? Explain.

4. Describe one or more *special* moments for you on your journey of *Finding Love* in the New Testament? Was there an *overall* way of understanding *love* that stands out for you? Or were there simply some *moments* that especially caught your attention or influenced you?

5. Was it important for you to learn that *agapē* love does not occur on the lips of Paul in the Acts of the Apostles in the New Testament? If so, why was it important? If not, why not?

6. What is your response to the idea that Paul evidently did not use *love* language in his day-to-day activities with people in his business of tentmaking but probably was influenced by the *communal* experience of writing letters to include language about *love*?

Books for Further Reading

Bondi, Roberta C. *To Pray and to Love: Conversations on Prayer with the Early Church.* Minneapolis: Fortress, 1991.

> Roberta C. Bondi is Professor Emerita at Candler School of Theology at Emory University in Atlanta, Georgia. She is a Methodist theologian and church historian. In this book she draws on the riches of early monastic writers to write a book on prayer that is loving and wise. She invites us to keep company with early Christian writers to show us a way to pray, think, and live reciprocally in God's love.

Carter, Warren. *Seven Events that Shaped the New Testament World.* Grand Rapids: Baker Academic, 2013.

> Warren Carter is the LaDonna Kramer Meinders Professor of New Testament at Phillips Theological Seminary in Tulsa, Oklahoma, with a PhD from Princeton Theological Seminary. Chapter two in this book presents an outstanding account of the translation of the Hebrew Scriptures into Greek as one of the major events that shaped the New Testament world. The final portion of the chapter discusses multiple places in the New Testament where the Greek Old Testament provided a special lens for interpreting the story of Jesus as God's Messiah.

Fowl, Stephen E. *Theological Interpretation of Scripture: Classic and Contemporary Readings.* Eugene, OR: Cascade Books, 2009.

> Stephen E. Fowl is President and Dean of Church Divinity of the Pacific, in Berkeley, California. He is a distinguished theologian and highly regarded lay leader in the Episcopal Church who previously was Professor of Theology at Loyola University Maryland in Baltimore. This book presents rich insights into journeying spiritually with profound and deeply informed reading of Scripture.

Jackson, Timothy P. *Political Agape: Christian Love and Liberal Democracy.* Grand Rapids: Eerdmans, 2015.

> Timothy P. Jackson is Professor of Christian ethics and Senior Research Fellow at Candler School of Theology and the Center for the Study of Law and Religion at Emory University in Atlanta, Georgia. In this book he asks, "What is the place of Christian love in a pluralistic society dedicated to liberty and justice for all." What would it mean to take both Jesus Christ and Abraham Lincoln seriously and attempt to translate love of God and neighbor into every quarter of life, including law and politics?

Jobes, Karen H., and Moisés Silva. *Invitation to the Septuagint.* 2nd ed. Grand Rapids, Baker Academic, 2015.

> Karen H. Jobes is Gerald F. Hawthorne Professor Emerita of New Testament Greek and Exegesis at Wheaton College and Graduate School and Moisés Sylva has taught biblical studies at Westmont College, Westminster Theological Seminary, and Gordon-Conwell Theological Seminary and now lives in Litchfield, Michigan. This book is a user-friendly introduction to the Greek Old Testament that was groundbreaking in its first edition. The second edition presents the most up-to-date scholarship in an informed and accessible style that introduces the general reader to some of the most recent developments in this exciting and recently developing field of study and interpretation.

Lewis, C. S. *The Four Loves.* London: Bles, 1960.

> C. S. Lewis was an Anglican lay theologian who held academic positions in English literature at both Oxford University and Cambridge University until his death in 1963. This book on *The Four Loves* is a classic exploration of the four types of human love, which he names as affection, friendship, erotic love, and the love of God. Throughout this compassionate and reasoned study, he encourages readers to open themselves to all forms of love as a key to understanding that brings us closer to God.

Books for Further Reading

Oord, Thomas Jay. *Defining Love: A Philosophical, Scientific, and Theological Engagement*. Grand Rapids: Brazos, 2010.

> In this book, Thomas Jay Oord, who directs doctoral programs at Northwind Theological Seminary and directs the Center for Open and Relational Theology, introduces the worlds of science and theology to a new field of integrative research and conceptualization that gives *agape* a new centrality in our lives. He shows that science supports the best in Christian teaching, and he offers his own richly nuanced doctrine of love, involving God's love for the world and our love for God and our fellow creatures to which we are called. This book brings a strong voice to current questions about divine power, the gift, creation, and cosmology.

Oord, Thomas Jay. *The Nature of Love: A Theology*. St. Louis, MO: Chalice, 2010.

> Thomas Jay Oord directs doctoral programs at Northwind Theological Seminary and directs the Center for Open and Relational Theology. He is a theologian, philosopher, and scholar of multidisciplinary studies. This book is an exploration of a theology of love that carefully, critically, and creatively engages some of the giants of Christian tradition such as Augustine and Aquinas, Anders Nygren and Clark H. Pinnock, Karl Barth, and John Cobb. He crafts his own distinctive vision of Love Divine in a rich celebration of a Christ-centered theology of "essential kenosis," *divine emptying*, that has profound implications for the breadth and depth of Christian doctrine.

Nygren, Anders. *Agape and Eros: The Christian Idea of Love*. Translated by Philip S. Watson. Chicago: University of Chicago Press, 1982.

> Anders Nygren was a Swedish Lutheran theologian who was Professor of Systematic Theology at Lund University from 1924 and was elected Bishop of Lund in 1948. This is a classic two-volume work published as one volume in this University of Chicago Press edition. Part One (the first volume) examines *eros* and *agape* in Greek philosophy and the New Testament. Part Two (the second volume) explores *eros* and *agape* in the Apostolic Fathers and Apologists, Gnosticism, Marcion, Tertullian, and Alexandrian Theology before turning to Augustine, Plotinus, and writers during the Middle Ages. After a chapter on Martin Luther and the Reformation, the book ends with a discussion of "How Agape-Love Is Built Up."

Books for Further Reading

Outka, Gene. *Agape: An Ethical Analysis.* New Haven: Yale University Press, 1972.

> Gene H. Outka was Dwight Professor Emeritus of Philosophy and Christian Ethics at Yale University until his death on May 1, 2023. This book examines and discusses Roman Catholic and Protestant writings on *agape* from the emergence of Anders Nygren's *Agape and Eros* in 1930 through its influence in the writings of thinkers like M. C. D'Arcy, Reinhold Niebuhr, Paul Ramsey, Paul Tillich, and Karl Barth. The chapters discuss Human Love, Self-Love, Justice, Subsidiary Rules, Agape as a Virtue, Justification, Equal Regard, Self-Sacrifice, and Mutuality. This is a remarkable book on religious ethics that brings together analytic moral philosophy and theological ethics. At the time of its publication, many considered it perhaps the best available book about contemporary Christian ethical theory.

Park, Song-Mi Suzie. *Love in the Hebrew Bible.* Louisville: Westminster John Knox, 2023.

> This is a wonderful companion volume to the present one on love in the New Testament. Suzie Park is Associate Professor of Old Testament at Austin Presbyterian Seminary in Austin, Texas. Through a discussion of stories and poems, she explains unique ancient cultural understandings of loving and being loved and how perspectives on love were intertwined with ancient Israelite conceptions of kinship, gender, and politics. In the Hebrew Bible love can be sweet, beautiful, and joyous, or it can be jealous and violent. It can also be political, public, covenantal, and physical.

Peckham, John C. *The Concept of Divine Love in the Context of the God–World Relationship.* Studies in Biblical Literature 159. New York: Lang, 2015.

> John C. Peckham is Associate Professor of Theology and Christian Philosophy at the Theological Seminary of Andrews University, Berrien Springs, Michigan. This book addresses the significant and far-reaching theological conflict over the nature of God's love, which he perceives to be deeply rooted in broader conflicts regarding the nature of divine being and the relation of God to the world. Peckham presents an extensive investigation of the entire biblical canon to present a comprehensive, logical approach that yields fresh conclusions for us in our present world.

Books for Further Reading

Schroff, Laura, and Alex Tresniowski. *An Invisible Thread: The True Story of an 11-Year-Old Panhandler, A Busy Sales Executive, and an Unlikely Meeting with Destiny.* New York: Howard, 2011.

> This book presents a true story of Laura Schroff, a successful ad sales representative in Manhattan, New York, who walked by but then walked back to a homeless, eleven-year-old panhandler on the street who had asked her for spare change. After this first encounter, they met up nearly every week for years as she took him to places to eat and finally even to her home, giving him clothes and other necessities for his family. This is an amazing story of love-in-action that has the potential to inspire even the least of us to find more ways to enact generosity in our daily lives alongside people less fortunate than we are.

Wischmeyer, Oda. *Love as Agape: The Early Christian Concept and Modern Discourse.* Translated by Wayne Coppins. Waco, TX: Baylor University Press, 2021.

> Oda Wischmeyer is Professor Emerita of Ancient Judaism and New Testament at University of Erlangen, Germany. This book shows how the Christian concept of love is rooted in Israel's scriptures, relates to ancient philosophical discourse, and came to have a definitive impact on western civilization. This book has revitalized a discussion of the divine yet socially embodied love of God in Christ. She argues that love is more than an ethical value. Rather, it is foundational to a Christian conception of God and a major catalyst for community formation in both the past and the present.

www.ingramcontent.com/pod-product-compliance
Lightning Source LLC
Chambersburg PA
CBHW031500160426
43195CB00010BB/1052